Along the Way *Series*
With Gary and Anne Marie Ezzo

Preparation for Parenting - Along the Infant Way
Preparation for the Toddler Years - Along the Toddler Way
Growing Kids God's Way - Along the Virtuous Way
Parenting the Middle Years - Along the Middle Years Way
Reaching the Heart of Your Teen - Along the Adolescent Way
Reflections of Moral Innocence - Along the Innocent Way

Parenting The Middle Years

Nurturing Your Eight to Twelve Year Old

Along the Middle Years Way

Gary & Anne Marie Ezzo

Parenting The Middle Years
Nurturing Your Eight to Twelve Year Old

© 1996, 2002, 2007 Gary and Anne Marie Ezzo

International Standard Book Number
ISBN-10: 1-883035-04-X
ISBN-13 978-1-883035-04-4

Printed in the United States of America

Growing Families International
2160 Cheswick Lane, Mt. Pleasant, South Carolina 29466

07 08 09 10 11 — 12 11 10 9 8

Dedicated to:

Cliff and Wilma Olson
who graciously guided us
through the middle years

Acknowledgements

No book is really written by a single author. Neither was this one. We owe a special debt of gratitude to a host of families who prayed us through the completion of this series. We want to acknowledge John and Holly Angle, Greg and Diane Roehr, and Tim and Kathy Lambros for sharing their common sense insights that added to the practical side of this book. We also wish to offer a special thanks to Jeff and Sharon Secor for their ministry commitment to single parents who are working through the preadolescent transition as well as Jim Bennett for his assistance in our Courtship chapter. We wish to thank Pastor Robert Boerman for his theological suggestions and contributions. Also to Liz Sykes for her wonderful review of the text and editorial suggestions. And last, but not least, a special word of thanks to all those *Growing Kids God's Way* parents who, with the blessings of God, helped us pioneer the moral revolution so many years ago. To all of you: thanks for being a message of hope to a watching world.

Table of Contents

Preface

We wrote the this series soon after completing our first edition of the *Reaching the Heart of Your Teen* series, (1995). It was then we realized the need for such a preparatory middle years teaching for the age period of eight to twelve years old. The many conversations with desperate mothers and fathers relationally struggling with their teens convinced us that most of the storm and stress experienced could have been minimized, if not prevented altogether, if only these parents had some practical guidance a few years earlier.

Rightly meeting the small challenges along the middle years way reduces the likelihood of big challenges in the teen years. The period between eight to twelve years of age finds children in three major transitions – moral, biological, and social. Each transition brings its own set of adjustments, conflicts, and changes. Yes, changes. Your children are growing up and that means you must grow with them.

The middle years awaken within a child a sense of fearful adventure in an ever-expanding world outside the security and confines of Mom and Dad. It is the first phase in the transition from dependence on parents to the self-reliance of adulthood. Therefore, this transition must be accompanied by patience, understanding, and plenty of parental faith in the belief that He who has begun a good work in you will continue it in your children.

Parenting the Middle Years is the logical extension of *Growing Kids God's Way*. In that series, the prerequisites for this next parenting installment were established. For example, we are assuming that you are giving your children the "moral reason why" as we taught you in Chapter One of *Growing Kids God's Way*. We are assuming that you are still doing couch time as described in "Right Beginnings" (Chapter Two). We are assuming you are speaking your child's love language as we taught you in "Touchpoints of Love" (Chapter Three), and that each dad is fulfilling his obligation listed in the "Father's Mandate" (Chapter Four). We assume you are continually developing godly character both by your instruction and example (chapters six through eight). We are assuming you have a handle on the discipline issues facing your children (Chapters Nine through Sixteen). These are just some of the actions we are assuming are routinely going on in your house.

Before bringing this introduction to a close, there are some "housekeeping" details to alert you to. This workbook is incomplete without the corresponding video or audio tapes. There are six video sessions. Each session is divided into two segments, both approximately thirty minutes long. The split session allows those who choose to use the Sunday School hour to complete this series, allowing more time for discussion. (Obviously, approaching the series in thirty-minute segments will extend the length of the course beyond six weeks.) Each video session corresponds to a chapter (or chapters) in this workbook. The match-up is as follows:

Session One
Part 1   Chapter One
          Welcome Back

Part 2   Chapter Two
          The Invisible Role of Authority

Session Two
Part 1   Chapter Three
          Adolescence and Maturity

Part 2   Chapter Four
          Understanding Moral Maturity

Session Three
Part 1   Chapter Five
          Influences on Behavior

Part 2   Chapter Six
          The Power of Groupthink

Session Four
Part 1   Chapter Seven
          Communication and Conversation

Part 2   Chapter Seven
          Communication and Conversation .

Session Five
Part 1   Chapter Eight
          How to Encourage

Part 2   Chapter Nine
          Discipline Potpourri

Session Six
Part 1   Chapter Ten
          Dating and Courtship

Part 2   Chapter 11
          Seven Warning Flags

Your standing homework assignment is to read the corresponding chapter(s) and answer the study questions at the end of each one.

There are also three matters of terminology to point out. First, we used both genders "he" and "she" throughout the book because the principles presented work equally well with both genders. Second, we interchange the singular pronoun "I" and the plural pronoun "we" throughout the text. The first ("I") refers to Gary's narrative, and the second to the collective insights of both Gary and Anne Marie. A third matter deals with the title *Growing Kids God's Way.* We often used the initials *GKGW* in its place or, *Growing Kids*, which has now become a popular folk title of the program.

If we learned anything from teaching frustrated parents battling their teenagers, it is this: the "middle years," more than the teen years, is the crucible in which preparation for responsible living is established. The next fifteen hundred days are all you have to prepare your kids for the nearly thirty-seven hundred days of adolescence. Are you ready?

Gary and Anne Marie
Charleston, South Carolina 2002

1

Welcome Back

We start this series with two truths: First, parenting is a process leading to maturity. Who of us was mature enough to have children before our children came? It seems that marriage is not solely blessed because it produces children, but that our children are part of the process helping produce two mature beings – Mom and Dad. Second, nothing of value comes quickly. That "great family" with the "great kids" living down the street didn't just happen. And no intimate relationship sustains itself over a long time without a few waves, storms, and course corrections.

The middle years is a time of realignment and sometimes course correction for children and parents. These are transition years when children start the long process of metamorphosis – moving away from childhood dependencies and interests, and moving toward healthy independence and self-responsibility. It is a period marked by a greater sensitivity to the differences between self and peers. There is a growing interest in what the group thinks. As peer influence begins to challenge the status quo of behavior, children begin to measure themselves against the norms of the group. What is the group wearing, listening to, doing,

and where are they going?

The endocrine system begins to release potent hormones nudging boys and girls to sexual awareness. Now, sons and daughters begin to change their minds about the opposite sex and start, all of a sudden, to view the other gender as something attractive. More attention is paid to hygiene and grooming with a heightened sensitivity to appearance and dress.

The middle years is a time of great moral and intellectual growth, when a child begins to take ownership of his own values and beliefs. It is a time when the world opens up to him and when the meaning of life beyond Mom and Dad's design begins to take shape. Yes, it is a time of great transition. But it is a transition for both parent and child.

MARKS OF A HEALTHY FAMILY

What are the marks of healthy families? While experiences differ and no one has universal insights, we maintain that healthy family relationships are cultivated, not inherited. Here is a list of traits common to healthy *Growing Kids God's Way* families. Healthy families:

1. Have a core of shared values that all members embrace.

2. Know how to communicate with each other.
3. Have parents who are not afraid to say, "I was wrong."
4. Have teens who are willing to accept "no" for an answer.
5. Have parents who are approachable about their own sin.
6. Maintain the marriage as a recognized priority of family health.
7. Make time to be with each other and to attend each other's events.
8. Have parents who are not afraid of the teen years.
9. Have teens who are confident of their parents' trust in them.
10. Have members who are loyal to each other.
11. Have planned family events.
12. Elevate conflict resolution above conflict avoidance.
13. Have a corporate sense of responsibility to all members.
14. Swap family rules for family courtesies as the child matures.
15. Act on the belief that the family unit is more important than the individual.

Don't assume that healthy families are without problems. They aren't! Stress, trials, conflicts, financial problems, and sinful attitudes confront healthy families as much as they do unhealthy ones. The difference is this: healthy families know how to deal with stress. and draw upon each other's strengths to get through their trials. They know how to resolve conflict instead of avoiding it. They know how to confess their faults to one another.

HEALTHY FAMILY PROFILE
Having listed the traits of healthy families, how is your family doing? What is the status of your family's health? The following questions are designed to assess that very question. Take the test for each middle years child. The table of norms found at the conclusion of the test represents actual readings from healthy families whose public reputation includes having courteous children and a close family identity, as well as families struggling in various aspects of their relationship.

We designed this test to provide an objective point of reference. Your score will help evaluate where you stand when compared to the two groups mentioned above. The test is not meant to encourage or discourage parents (although both may happen) but to provide a starting point for improvement. No one needs to see your score, so please consider each question carefully. Honestly evaluate the overall characterization of your child's behavior before marking down your answer.

The test is divided into two sections, each with its own rating scale. When you complete both sections, add the scores, total the results, and mark the score on page 12. If for some reason a question does not apply, make an educated guess. For personal enlightenment, consider taking the test on behalf of your own parents. How do you think they would answer these questions about you? (You may duplicate this test if used with this series.)

Section One
Write in your responses adjacent to each question in this section and rate the questions using a 1 to 5 scale.

1 = This is very representative of our child or our relationship.
2 = This is usually representative of our child or our relationship.

3 = Sometimes this is true of our child or our relationship, but just as often it is not.

4 = This is not usually true of our child or our relationship.

5 = This rarely, if ever, is true of our child or our relationship.

1. _3_ If our preadolescent was at a neighbor's house and there was a questionable television program or movie on, my child would either call home to find out if it was okay or not watch it.

2. _3_ Our preadolescent is characterized by first and second levels of initiative as described in *GKGW*.

3. _2_ Our preadolescent is characterized by the same level of behavior outside our presence as when he/she is with us.

4. _1_ If my preadolescent has been in trouble away from us, he/she would come and tell us before we found out from someone else.

5. _23_ My preadolescent is beginning to pursue his/her own relationship with God.

6. _15_ If my preadolescent sees a piece of paper on the floor, even if he/she didn't drop it, he/she would be characterized by picking it up.

7. _2_ At this age, our preadolescent knows the moral reason why for most instructions we give.

8. _5_ Our preadolescent is characterized by using the appeal process.

9. _2_ Our preadolescent considers his/her siblings as part of his/her inner circle of best friends.

10. _1_ For his or her age, my preadolescent is wise to the world but not worldly wise.

11. _1_ Our preadolescent looks forward to special family times when it is just us together.

12. _3_ Our preadolescent can accept "no" for an answer without blowing up.

13. _23_ Our preadolescent knows that if we wrong him/her in any way, he/she can count on an apology from us.

14. _4_ Our preadolescent picks up after himself or herself.

15. _2_ In our family, we practice seeking forgiveness from one another rather than just saying, "I'm sorry."

Section One Score   _39_

Section Two

Writing in your responses on the blanks adjacent to each question in this section, rate the questions using a 5 to 1 scale.

5 = Always true, or this is very representative of our teen, his/her feelings, our feelings, or our relationship.

4 = Often the case, or this is usually representative of our teen, his/her feelings, our feelings, or our relationship.

3 = Sometimes this is true, but just as often it is not.

2 = This happens, but not often. Or, this is not usually representative of my teen, his/her feelings, our feelings, or our relationship.

1 = This is rarely, if ever, true of our teen or our relationship.

1. _1_ Our preadolescent seems to have a split personality. He acts one way when he is with us, but is not as

yielding to authority when at school or church.

2. _#2_ Our preadolescent is jealous and pouts when something good happens to a sibling but does not happen to him/her.

3. _3_ We seem to be tightening the boundaries more than loosening them now that our child is in the middle years.

4. _#2_ We are beginning to notice that peers are having a greater negative influence on our preadolescent's attitudes than we are having a positive influence on his/her attitudes.

5. _5_ We are always reminding our preadolescent to pick up after himself or herself.

6. _2_ When we ask our preadolescent to do something, we always end up in a power struggle.

7. _1_ Worldly, trendy fashions are becoming a source of conflict between our preadolescent and ourselves.

8. _2_ Our preadolescent seems to frequently take advantage of siblings.

9. _3_ Our preadolescent gets angry when things don't go his or her way.

10. _2_ Our preadolescent seems to make impetuous decisions without thought of future consequences.

11. _____ Our preadolescent will do something good to get out of doing what he or she was told.

12. _2_ Our preadolescent will tell us a partial truth or openly lie to us rather than admit irresponsibility.

13. _3 4_ Our preadolescent is never satisfied with just "no." He always has to ask a series of challenging "whys."

14. _1_ Even if we were just going next door, I don't think I could trust leaving my preadolescent alone for an hour.

15. _1_ Our preadolescent tends to be drawn to the kids who are always getting in trouble rather than the good kids who stay out of trouble.

Section Two Score   _31_
Score from Section One   _35_
Total   _74_

Middle Years Healthy Family Profile Summary

30 – 45   Healthy, right on track, need to fine tune some issues.

46 – 60   Healthy, basically on track, working on some issues.

61 – 75   There are a number of behavioral concerns that if not corrected can lead to struggles and conflict during adolescence.

76 – 90   There are too many negative patterns signaling course correction is needed immediately.

91 – 150 Seriously off course. Get back into *GKGW*.

Name of child _Mavin – 2009_
    Score _____

Name of child _Elsie 2009_
    Score _____

Name of child _____
    Score _____

2

The Invisible Role of Authority

Discipline is a process of training and learning. It comes from the word disciple – one who is a learner. Children are not endowed at birth with self-control, nor is your pre-toddler, toddler, or young child experienced enough in life to know how to morally discipline himself (Proverbs 29:15b). Parents fulfill that role as teachers, while children are disciples who learn from them a way of life (Proverbs 1:8-9). The learning process requires the use of parental authority. For without it, you cannot lead, guide, and direct the child in the way of the Lord. For if there is no back pressure to bring about moral compliance, compliance will not happen.

In *Growing Kids God's Way*, we discussed the importance of parental authority in the home. It is not our intention to revisit all that was said in that series, but to begin a new conversation about the decreasing role that parental authority plays in the life of preteens and teens.

To move forward with this discussion, we first need to review the differences between biblical obedience (which calls for the use of parental authority) and submission (which signals a voluntary yielding). Obedience (from the Greek word *hupakouo*, meaning to line up under) is used in Scripture for children, slaves, soldiers, and servants. It is an implied mandate – a moral obligation. It is a duty command. Obedience is something you *have* to do. Submission is something you *want* to do. The word *submission* (from the Greek word *hupotasso*) also means to line up under but represents a different motive for compliance. Instead of obeying out of duty, *hupotasso* suggests submitting out of a devotional loyalty. The word is used for wives in Ephesians 5:22 and speaks of a devotional submission.

Establishing right motives for right behavior is one of the primary goals of child training. You want to move your child to the place where he will do right out of loyalty devotion to you (God's representatives) and not out of duty. You want voluntary submission, in time, to replace the necessary coerced obedience.

AUTHORITY AND INFLUENCE

What would you rather lead your preteen and teen by: the power of your authority or the strength of your relational influence? The first is related to obedience, the second is associated with a child's devotional submission. Managing or mismanaging parental leadership can make all the difference as to how peaceful or turbulent the teen years will be for your family.

We want to spend the rest of this chapter talking about parental authority – more specifically, how not to abuse it. By the time your children approach the teen years, you should be well on your way to leading them by the strength of your relational influence. This means the power of your authority, once used to control and direct your child's outward behavior, should begin to be less needed. Take note of our diagram. The simple rule is this: The younger the child the more you will guide and direct by your authority. The older the child, the more you should guide and direct by the strength of your relational influence.

Write out our own family moral code

Authority has always been a struggle for humankind. From birth, children struggle with it, and as we grow older it doesn't get any easier. Some people can't seem to live with it, yet most of us understand that you can't live harmoniously without it.

In the Christian family, the Bible not only provides the basis of all authority but also the ethics governing the exercise of authority. Biblical authority is beautiful because it is morally focused. Similar to the character of love (1 Corinthians 13:5-7), biblical authority is not presumptuous, proud, unkind, or unfair but full of integrity, gentle, consistent, and gracious. It's motivated by love and used only

when needed. Its purpose is to guide by encouragement and restraint. Authority is necessary because law and order for the family and the society is dependent on its proper administration. But authority can be taken to extremes. Too much authority leads to totalitarianism, while insufficient authority leads to injustice and social chaos.

In societal settings, whether it be a nation of families or a single family, the amount of rules, regulations, and authority needed to govern a people is determined by the moral consensus of the people. Moral consensus refers to values mutually agreed upon that govern individual behavior for the common good. The more values we share in common as a community of people, the less there is a need for coercive government to bring social order. In contrast, the more individual values conflict with societal values, the more intrusive government must become to insure social harmony. That same law of social order applies to our families.

What we are striving for in our homes is social order and unity without coercive authority, especially when there is a preteen or teenager living in the house. In order to achieve that end, we must balance the need for parental authority with a child's growing sense of personal responsibility. The closer the family draws to agreed upon values, the less there is a need for rulership by authority.

THE AUTHORITY EXCHANGE

Are you using more or less of your authority now that your children are in the middle years? We hope it's less. As children approach adolescence, the need for *parental rule* should decline in direct proportion to the child's increased rate of *moral self-rule*. The word *moral* in the previous sentence is operative.

The ontological fact that children are born with the natural propensity for selfish self-rule dates back to Cain and Abel. Children are born self-oriented; biblical ethics is other-oriented. The tension between the two creates conflicts that must be resolved by parental leadership.

By their authority, parents direct their children to virtuous behavior, reinforcing compliance by extrinsic means until the child is morally mature enough to govern himself by intrinsic values. This explanation assumes a decreasing emphasis on leadership by authority and an increasing emphasis on leadership by influence. That is, the older a child becomes, the less you lead by your authority and the more you lead by your relational influence.

By the time a child reaches the middle years, he should be well on his way to having acquired a moral code to which he voluntarily adheres with increasing frequency. The more he voluntarily yields to that code, the less parental authority is needed – but equally so, the more parental example is required.

A child who has been taught that it is wrong to lie and who attempts to be honest will lack encouragement to continue with honesty if he does not see his parents living honestly. Hearing a parent violating the truth of a conversation, or hearing a father describing some dubious business deal, or telling his wife when the phone rings, "If it is for me, tell them, I'm not home" chips away at the honesty message and undermines parental integrity.

The inconsistency between values preached and values lived will always force a greater need for parental policing, than would have been necessary if parents themselves were greater examples of the virtues they are trying to instill.

INVISIBLE AUTHORITY

As you approach your child's adolescence, you want your authority to become invisible. Looking at the various phases of development will help demonstrate this point.

Let's start at infancy. Infancy is the zenith of parental authority. This is when all of life's decisions are made by Mom and Dad. They determine when the child will eat, sleep, stay awake, have a bath, play on the blanket, or go for a stroller ride. Such tight supervision is absolutely necessary at this age, since the child simply does not have the moral conscience or intellect to know what is best and what is needed.

Now consider parental authority in the life of a five year old. By five, a child has gained some internal mastery over his life and actions, and that mastery allows him a degree of corresponding freedom. The decreased need of parental authority is proportionate to the increased amounts of age-appropriate, self-imposed controls. Please note that parental authority does not diminish, but rather the need for its use does.

For example, there are some activities in a five year old's day that no longer need Mom or Dad's direct approval. A five year old can come and go from the back yard, pick out his own board games, play with his hamster, or go to his room and play with a puzzle. While there is a gate preventing his one-year-old brother from access to the upstairs bedroom, the five year old navigates the barrier without need of parental approval. Why? Because such approval is assumed. Because the child continually demonstrated responsible behavior in these areas, parental policing is not necessary. Our point is this: Although parental authority is still a considerable influence in a five year old's life, it is not as sweeping in its control as it was a few years earlier.

How about the child at ten? Because of his increased ability for sustained periods of healthy self-rule, the need for visible authority is substantially reduced. A ten year old should be rapidly approaching moral maturity. Again, it is not that Mom and Dad's authority is no longer valid, but that the need for external control is diminishing. Gradually, parental control is being replaced by parental influence, and extrinsic motivation governing the child's life is replaced by intrinsic beliefs ruling from his heart.

Now we come to the teen years – the time you should be striving for moral consensus through moral maturity. Internalized virtues within the heart of the child should be ruling, not coercive parental authority. Moral maturity emancipates the child, allowing him to direct his own behavior. The good news for you is that such emancipation does not mean your child will leave the security of the home or reject your values. Your child during every phase of growth needs love, security, and understanding from the two most important people in his life – Mom and Dad.

Possessing the moral maturity that we're talking about does not mean your teen is all-knowing spiritually, but it does mean he knows and lives the "otherness" standards of Scripture. Moral maturity connects parents and teens at the heart with common character traits, mutual respect, and honor. Yet, at the same time, both maintain the uniqueness of their God-given relationship as children and parents.

SOME FINAL THOUGHTS

When we speak of leading by your influence not your authority, we want to make clear that we are not suggesting that you eliminate house or family rules. Your preteens and teens are still accountable to you, and there are community tasks and responsibilities that need to be maintained. Someone still needs to take out the trash, make his own bed, clean up after himself, be home at a reasonable hour, and yes, comply with parental instruction. What we are saying is that the basic tasks of life should take on new meaning – a moral one in response to a relationship to the family and not simply a response to some cold and impersonal set of rules reinforced by coercive authority.

Parental authority should not disappear during the teen years but should be used as a backup to enforce times of non-compliance. The majority of your leadership and your teen's response to it should be based on a new level of cooperation that calls him to live responsibly within the confines of the community called "family."

Our children will always be our children, and we their parents. But sooner or later they will grow into moral maturity, no longer requiring the parental policing of their behavior. What we are advocating is this: the sooner the better.

By that last statement, we aren't asking you to abdicate your role or responsibilities as a parent, nor are we suggesting that you should let your preteen or teen go wherever his passions lead him. But we are saying adolescence is a time when your child is best served when you lead by your influence and strength of relationship, rather than by the power of your authority. The truth is, once your kids hit the teen years, your relationship – good or bad – is the greatest asset or liability you have.

Questions for Review

1. Contrast "obedience" and "submission."

2. What is meant by the following statement: "Establishing right motives for right behavior is one of the primary goals of child training"?

3. Why is parental authority needed in the early years of training?

4. In your own words, summarize the main points of this chapter.

3

Just Ahead: Adolescence and Maturity

Every species, whether animal or human, follows a pattern of development peculiar to that species. That is God's design. For every human adult, there was a period of eight or nine years when that person was no longer a child but not yet an adult. Adolescence is the term used to designate this in-between period of life. The word is derived from the Latin verb *adolescere*, which means to ripen or to grow into maturity. Adolescence is the period of growth when the characteristics of childhood are gradually exchanged for those of adulthood – a time when a child is not firmly established in either category.

There is a difference between the terms *adolescent* and *teen*. The word "teen" (or "teenager") is derived from the numerical age span of thirteen to nineteen years, while "adolescent" is a broader term. A child enters adolescence with the onset of puberty, which occurs between ten and twelve years of age, and ends with physical maturity, usually attained between the years of nineteen and twenty-one.

The Bible doesn't use the terms "adolescent," "adolescence," or "teenager," but refers to children of this approximate age as *youth* or *young men*. For example, Daniel, Shadrach, Meshach, and Abed-Nego were all "young men" when taken to Babylon to serve Nebuchadnezzar (Daniel 1:3-4). Bible scholars place their ages between twelve and fifteen years. David is thought to have been about this same age when he fought Goliath as a "youth" (1 Samuel 17:42).

Regardless of which term is used – "teenager," "adolescent," "young man," or "youth" each of these words represents essentially the same period of growth and development. In this series, we will use the terms interchangeably and use them in the context of our society.

4- LEVELS OF ADOLESCENT MATURITY

Is adolescence a necessary period of growth leading to maturity, or an unnecessary extension of childhood? Some clinicians believe the latter and suggest that adolescence is an artificial secondary stage of development thrust upon twentieth-century man by the industrial revolution. As such, it only serves to delay maturity in children by slowing their entrance into adulthood. The *myth of adolescence*, as this view is commonly referred to, presupposes that children today are capable of moving into the adult community much sooner than what society allows, and to delay their entrance only fosters rebellion.

But in order to exist, this view forces a redefinition of the words maturity and adulthood by removing them from their normative, historical, biological, intellectual, and moral usage. Does a child become an adult when he matures, or does he mature when he becomes an adult? What is maturity, anyway? What does it look like? What is adulthood? Do all children go through adolescence and arrive at maturity at the same rate and time? Before we can put the challenge of preadolescence into perspective, we first must define the four levels of maturity – legal, physical, social/intellectual, and moral. How a society views these four levels of maturity highly influences how they view the preparation phase of adolescence.

Legal Maturity

When we say someone has reached the age of legal maturity, we mean that the person is old enough to participate in the full range of adult behavior permitted by law. Legal maturity is defined by time, not experience, and every nation determines its own legal customs and timetable for allowing an individual passage into the adult community.

For example, in America most states allow a sixteen year old the legal right to drive a car. But that same sixteen year old cannot legally vote until he is eighteen. He can legally play the California lottery as an eighteen year old, but he cannot legally buy alcoholic beverages until he is twenty-one. The point is this: legal maturity is progressive until twenty-one years of age, at which time full legal benefits and responsibilities are awarded to each member of society. Of course, as we all know, this right of passage does not necessarily signal a type of comprehensive maturity but rather society's declaration that a person is now a full member of the adult community.

Physical Maturity

Because all humans – of every tongue, tribe, and nation – demonstrate the same patterns of physical growth and development, physical maturation is reached at approximately the same time, eighteen to twenty years of age.

Physical growth is rapid during infancy and early childhood, followed by a slower pace just before puberty. A spurt of rapid growth follows puberty, extending into mid-adolescence. Growth then plateaus and begins to decelerate until adulthood. Between eighteen and twenty years of age, the skeletal growth process ends. This is marked by two events: the achievement of maximum body growth (height) and ossification of the sacral bones.

Physical maturity, then, is marked both by the *attainment of maximum growth* and the *cessation of growth*.

Social/Intellectual Maturity

Legal adulthood is fairly objective. A child reaches a prescribed age assigned by the society and he is declared "legally of age." This age in the United States is twenty-one. Physical maturity is also objectively observed by the attainment and cessation of growth common to all human beings. But in contrast to these first two, social/intellectual maturity has no such objective benchmark but is highly influenced by the nature and complexity of each society.

To explain this class of maturity, we'll begin by defining the terms *social maturity* and *intellectual maturity*. Social maturity refers to one's readiness to be an active participant in social policy affecting public welfare and the mutual good of the society at large. Intellectual maturity speaks to the minimum level of intellectual and academic attainment necessary to function in the adult community. From those two definitions comes the following single law of social order and adolescent development:

The level of social/intellectual maturity required before one can enter the adult community is determined by the simplicity or complexity of each society and the intellectual skills needed to participate as an adult member within the society.

Every society sets its own minimum social/intellectual standard to be met before a person is recognized as an adult. That basic law establishes for every society the length of time required to transition a child from childhood to adulthood. It is this law that determines and legitimizes the length of adolescence. Let's see how this basic law looks in four different cultural settings: primitive-tribal, pre-industrial America, postmodern America, and first-century Judaism.

PRIMITIVE-TRIBAL SOCIETIES

Anthropologists working with primitive tribes have noted the possibility that children in those environments can pass directly from childhood into adulthood without going through an adolescent phase. There is a practical reason for this. In such primitive settings, preparation for adulthood presents few of the social, intellectual, or moral challenges that are common to advanced societies. We have personally witnessed this social/intellectual phenomenon in primitive settings. Many of the skills needed to participate in the adult community – for example, fishing, hunting, and crop planting – are actually gained before the onset of puberty. These basic life skills represent higher education in these settings.

Primitive simplicity does not move children into adulthood earlier but brings adult status closer in age to childhood. It's the nature and degree of social complexity that determines the need for, and duration of, adolescence. In primitive settings, there is no need for a period of extended adolescence. This last point is further demonstrated by examining adolescence in pre-industrial America.

Prior to the American industrial revolution, children entered adulthood much later than children living in remote jungle villages but much earlier than children living in the 1990's. The reason? The social and intellectual skills needed to participate as an adult a hundred years ago were far less demanding than today. For example, back in my grandmother's day at the turn of the twentieth century, it was not uncommon for girls and boys to marry at fourteen or fifteen years of age and set up housekeeping. A sixteen year old marrying today, however, usually signals something altogether different. Today, you must be fifteen or sixteen in most states just to get a permit to begin learning to drive – with an experienced driver in the passenger seat.

A simpler life meant a simpler transition into adulthood and a shorter period of adolescence. This basic natural rule does not mean children back then matured sooner, but rather what was required for social and intellectual maturity was far less demanding than today. This point will be made more clear as we look at our current situation.

POSTMODERN AMERICA

The title, *postmodern America* is a relatively new societal classification that marks another level of social/intellectual advancement. Akin to this title is the *Age of Information*. This last title speaks to the volumes of current knowledge available to the average person. Both the volume and complexity of new information highly influences the length of adolescence in our day and pushes maturity back.

Today we live in an age of microchip technology. We talk of cyberspace, virtual reality, fiber optics, web sites, multi-tasking, and gigabytes. Adulthood in America, along with our European and Asian industrialized counterparts, requires the attainment of a variety of sophisticated skills and abilities unimagined just fifty years ago. The very complexity of the American adult life evokes a type of moratorium on early entry into adulthood. That's why a period of adolescent ripening is absolutely necessary in our current day. There is simply too much to learn.

Society does not have confidence to allow a fifteen year old to drive a bus, fly a commercial airliner, handle the rigors of an emergency room doctor, be a public school teacher, compete in the bond market, design bridges, build skyscrapers, or handle a thousand other intellectually demanding and skill-intensive jobs.

The intricacies of modern adulthood will not allow teenagers to participate on an equal footing with adults. Adolescents lack a type of wisdom and judgment that is gained through time with age and experience. The period of adolescence serves to better prepare our teens to compete with competency in the adult communities of our society and the world.

HISTORICAL JUDAISM

The "youth" phase in historical Judaism linked childhood with adulthood. It was a secondary phase very similar in nature to the adolescent phase found in preindustrial America. In Bible times, maturity was not synonymous with adulthood. That distinction is important to grasp. A minor reached "maturity" at thirteen, but adulthood came later, usually at around eighteen to twenty years of age. Maturity in the Hebrew culture spoke of a mixture of certain legal rights and moral obligations. It was a time when a child entered the adult world as a participant in religious and social ceremonies. The Jewish Bar Mitzvah (which refers to the time when one becomes a son of the Mosaic Law) served this purpose for boys. It marked the beginning of a youth's independent legal status and the age of moral responsibility. A youth could legally buy and trade in the marketplace, be a witness in court, even be married; but he was not "adult enough" to sell inherited real estate (the minimum age for such matters was eighteen), nor could he be a judge until he was twenty-one.

Keep in mind that Bar Mitzvah, although thoroughly Jewish, was not a biblical rite of passage into adulthood. That is, it was not an ordinance established by God that defines adulthood. But Numbers 14:29 does. This Old Testament passage is the only narrative in Scripture that speaks to the age of adult accountability. You may remember that God declared that those twenty years of age and older (except for Caleb and Joshua) would die in the wilderness for their sin of unbelief. The punishment was pronounced on the "adult population." Further evidence supporting the distinction between legal maturity and that of adulthood in a Jewish context is seen in the rare cases when youths (among whom physical signs of maturity had not appeared) were legally granted adult status at twenty years of age.

We will conclude this section by stating what we hope is now made clear: The cessation or even the necessity of adolescence is governed by the adult demands of the culture in which an individual lives. The simpler the society, the sooner a child moves into adulthood. The more complex, the longer is the adolescent transition. In our society, the period of adolescence is a necessary reality – one that should not be trivialized.

Moral Maturity

It perhaps is natural to think that moral maturity follows the same growth patterns as does legal, physical, social, and intellectual maturity. Many assume that, since a child tends to mature in each of these categories just before entrance to adulthood, personal moral-ity follows suit. This is not so. Such thinking delays moral maturity by removing the sense of urgency from parents of preadolescents. Childhood is the period for imparting moral instruction and directing moral training; but please note that adolescence is when principles of right living, thinking, and acting should be realized. That fact forms the basis of this entire curriculum and becomes the centerpiece of our conversation in Chapter Four.

Questions for Review

1. Explain the difference between the terms "adolescent" and "teenager."

2. What is the premise behind the "Myth of Adolescence"?

3. Explain why some cultures have an adolescent period and others do not.

4. In historical Judaism, what did Bar Mitzvah mark for boys?

4

Understanding Moral Maturity

In biblical context, moral maturity (thinking and acting in harmony with God's moral law), should show itself between the ages of thirteen and fifteen. That is our experience. Too often, parents of preadolescents misjudge the timing. They view adolescence as the period of moral ripening and not the time of moral living. Be warned, the pre-adolescence middle years are the last stop before moral patterns are lived out. Have you reached the heart of your child with the truth of God's Word? Are they learning the "one anothers" of Scripture and applying them to their own lives and family members? Are your children becoming sons and daughters of God's moral law?

We want you to think positively of the future. We want you to enjoy your adolescent adult. Adolescent adult? But how can a teenager be both an adolescent and an adult? This is an important concept to grasp because one principal factor to successful teen parenting is to have an adult relationship with your teen even though he or she is not yet an adult, physically, or intellectually. An adolescent adult is a teen who can relate morally on par with you. He or she possesses the moral graces in both conversation and action that attract appropriate attention.

Appropriate attention. We all know teens who attract inappropriate attention and some who attract no attention; but only morally mature teens attract appropriate attention. Attention is not drawn to themselves but to the quality of their character as demonstrated by the six categories of respect, including respect for authority, parents, elders, peers, property, and nature. When motivated by a devotion to God, these six shine forth as lights to the world (Matthew 5:16) and the sweet fragrance of salvation (2 Corinthians 2:14-15).

Biblical moral maturity is the only class of maturity that can put a young person on the same footing as an adult. Compatibility in relationship is enhanced by the common character traits of the heart. You want your preteen and teen to be your moral equal in these six categories long before he or she reaches adulthood physically, socially, or intellectually. The fact that adults and teens are both on the same page morally forms the basis of healthy family relationships.

OUR STORY

We discovered the benefits of moral maturity more by accident than design. Moving to southern California from northern New England in

1983 presented some challenges to the Ezzo family. At that time our children were twelve and fourteen years old. While waiting for housing to become available, we stayed with acquaintances for seven weeks (five weeks longer than we had planned). After two weeks of sharing intimate quarters and meals, plus laundry and housekeeping chores, our host commented: "All right. For two weeks now we have observed your girls. We know some kids can play at being good for a few days, but yours are continually joyful, obedient, and courteous. This is no facade. What makes them that way? What did you do?"

Not many weeks later another conversation was reported to us by a friend who overheard two teachers discussing the new students in their school. One teacher asked, "Have you met those two girls from New Hampshire? There is something wonderfully different about them."

Those two experiences, plus other gracious compliments about our daughters, prompted us to begin asking ourselves, *Why are they this way?* What had we done, either purposefully or inadvertently, to shape their early teen years? We certainly enjoyed our children, but equally important was the fact that other people enjoyed them. But what was it, exactly, that other people enjoyed about our daughters? What made adults feel comfortable around them? Why did young mothers want to sit and chat with them, or invite them out to lunch, and ask our teenage daughters questions about parenting, as if they were moms themselves? Why did other people enjoy our children?

Was it their physical maturity? No, it wasn't that; they were still teenagers needing more time to grow. Was it their academic or intellectual maturity and achievements? No, they both still had high school to complete, not to

mention college – there was plenty yet for them to learn. But there was something about Amy and Jennifer that put them on an equal footing with adults. What was it? It could only be one thing, we realized – their moral maturity. They had matured in the six categories of respect.

It was not just our kids. We have all met teens in their prime, who are known for being very sociable, courteous, respectful, gracious, motivated with helpful initiative, and very genuine. There are families all around us with teens of this moral caliber, where love and respect between parent and teen is evidenced by their mutual respect for one another and the absence of rebellious conflict. How did they get to this point of relational harmony? What is it about these kids that makes being with them enjoyable? What allows you to have fun with them, (and them with you) without having to default to a peer status with them? They have one common thread about them – a common moral maturity that makes them a pleasure to be with.

Children mature physically and intellectually at different rates. Yet it seems that in God's overall design of the four classes of maturity – legal, physical, intellectual, and moral – the one most tied to healthy human relationships is moral maturity; it is also, when nurtured correctly, the first to blossom. Biblical moral maturity is both the saving grace and construct of relational harmony for both family and society. In our next chapter we will look at the benefits of moral maturity.

VALUES-BASED PARENTING

Values govern every person's behavior. And to some extent our lives are marked by two sets of values: values based on what we believe (the ideal) and values based on what we do (the reality). The disparity between knowing godly values and living those values is the crux of the human dilemma and the source of many parent-child relational conflicts. Maybe it was this very point that James, the brother of our Lord wanted to get across to the Church when he said: "Be ye doers of the word and not hearers only deceiving yourselves," (James 1:22). As parents we need to be doers of what we know to be true, not just hearers.

When we as family members operate from the same values, the likelihood of family accidents at the intersections of our lives is drastically reduced. Why should you base your family relationships on biblical precepts? Here are some practical benefits.

Benefit 1: Parents Learn to Lead by Their Influence

A values-based approach to child rearing helps parents lead in such a way that their preteens and teens will follow. A common shoelace can help illustrate this principle. On a flat surface, stretch out a shoelace in front of you, one end nearer you (the "bottom") and the other end farther away (the "top"). Then place your finger at the bottom of the shoelace and begin pushing. What happens? The shoelace begins to stack up in loops and tangles as you push, but it does not move forward. In fact, the more you push, the more it twists and turns, moving in every direction but where you want it to go. Now take the other end of the shoe lace, the top, and begin pulling. What happens? You can lead the shoelace in any direction.

Many parents wish to move their teen-parent relationship from where it is to where it should be. But they find resistance because they are pushing from the bottom rather than leading from the top. They are attempting to force

change by the power of their authority, instead of leading by the power of their influence. Tis is such a critical concept to learn. Authority has limits, but influence knows no boundaries.

Benefit 2: It Morally Perfects Parents

It seems that God gives us children to perfect us. Have you noticed that? The moral relational approach forces all participating parents to improve their own moral proficiency. You must internalize the same biblical precepts that you require of your teen and live those precepts. Take honesty, for example. The ability to decide to be honest is the same whether a child makes it during a spelling test or an adult makes it when turning in an expense report. Moses, speaking of the moral statutes and precepts governing God's people in the new land, reminded parents that, "These things must first be in your heart" (Deuteronomy 6:6b). Parents must understand right and wrong before they can teach these principles to their children. But often God uses our children to force us to learn.

Benefit 3: Changes Are for a Lifetime

Values-based parenting governs relationships for a lifetime. Remember that truth. We are not offering a strategy just to get you through the teen years, but one that is life-long. The parent-child relationship is not bound by time, age, or some artificial social marker, such as high school or college graduation. Parent-child relationships are continuous. Today's teens, on average, can expect to live another fifty or sixty years. By God's grace, you also will live many of those years. What kind of relationship will you have with your child once he or she is out of the house? Your children will always be your children. There will always be a need for a healthy relationship.

Show, Expect them to follow don't tell

Benefit 4: Values-Based Parenting is Unifying

We know that family life, when established on a weak moral foundation, is threatened from the start. Where there are no common values there is no basis for family unity. If moral integrity is lacking or is allowed to sag or break down, the resulting strains will sooner or later produce relational conflict.

The "common-values" rule is this: the more each family member moves away from common moral ground, the more strain is placed on all relationships. The reverse is also true. With values-based parenting, a fixed set of otherness-values govern interpersonal relationships. A moral environment fosters a *we-ness* loyalty to one another.

The apostle Paul encouraged the Philippian brethren with these words: "Therefore if there is any consolation in Christ, if any comfort of love, if any fellowship of the Spirit, if any affection and mercy, fulfill my joy by being like-minded having the same love, being of one accord of one mind" (Philippians 2:1-2). Being like-minded, having the same love, and being of one accord – these attributes represent a noble goal for a Christian family. But how are they attained? Only through moral like-mindedness.

Benefit 5: The World Takes Notice

When God's values are allowed to dwell in you richly, the world will take notice. A desperate society will still be viewing the Christian message long after it stops listening to it. Do you see why this is true? In a society where natural family relationships are being destroyed, we, the Church, have the great opportunity to offer hope by our good behavior (Matthew 5:16b). When we keep our behavior pure, when we let our indwelling light shine forth – washing over our marriages, our children, our families, and our relationships with others – when we let the excellence of Christ be seen in our members, our conduct will not go unnoticed. The compelling testimony of our faith – as borne out by our actions – and the reality of the gospel, will stand in dramatic contrast to the negative consequences of other's poor choices (1 Peter 2:12). As a result, some of those in our midst will glorify God by accepting the gospel that we live before them.

THE BOTTOM LINE

Helping our children grow up with moral fortitude is the most important task of parenthood, apart from leading them to salvation. For whenever you introduce a child to God's moral law, you introduce him to the character of God. Our model, then, has two major components. First, parents must be both trustworthy and believable in the eyes of their children. And second, the child's heart must mature in biblical moral character.

This second requirement also begins with the parents. The planned outcome – the moral maturity of your child – assumes that the principles of right moral conduct are already present in your heart. The otherness sensitivity that we hope to develop in our children must first be part of our own character. In fact, our children usually will not advance any farther along the pathway to moral maturity than where we, their parents, are at any given time. Can you provide what your child needs for achieving moral maturity? If not, your house needs to be put in order. The following chapters will speak to the how-tos of this challenge.

Questions for Review

1. What is an adolescent adult?

2. As it relates to your children's character, what is appropriate attention?

3. What is the "common-values" rule?

4. How does values-based parenting morally perfect parents?

5

Influences on Behavior

The preadolescent is a child in transition from the relatively protected years of close parental supervision to the approaching and ever-expanding years of adolescence. During this transition period, the child begins to realize that he has a growing influence on others, and others outside of Mom and Dad are having a growing influence on him.

The theologian, J.M. Price once suggested to educators that to bring up a child properly, one needs to begin with grandparents. The implied meaning – children are a product of family influence. Whether that influence be hereditary, biological, or social, there are forces shaping beliefs and behaviors of every new generation. What are the influences in your preteen's life? Who are the influences? What can you do about them?

Over the next two chapters our discussion will center on the three primary influences that shape your preteen's world. First, there is the moral influence. Specifically we are referring to the quality of your child's moral understanding and commitment to family values. What is in your child's heart? Second, there are biological influences, which begin with puberty and end with maturity. Because of the influence of hormones, your child now views himself and

others differently, especially the "others" of the opposite sex. In our next chapter we will take up the third influence, that being the power of peer pressure and "groupthink." Your middle years child will learn what it means and what is required to belong to a group of peers and what it means to stand alone.

THE INFLUENCE OF MORALITY

As stated in Chapter Two, your middle years child should be well on his way to having acquired a set of personal values to which he adheres with increasing frequency. In the Christian home, moral adherence is dependent upon three factors: moral knowledge (what does God's moral law say?), moral reason (what does the law mean?), and last but certainly not least, parental example (how valid is the law in the life of those insisting on it?).

If these three steps can be achieved with your kids, then the great family down the street, with the great teenagers, will be yours. Why? Because the greatest influence on relationships is the values of the heart. Common values unify; conflicting values war against intimate healthy relationships, especially in the teen years.

So we ask you: What is in your child's heart? Who has shaped his or her morality? For the

Christian, true biblical morality has two components. First, our God is an ethical God and our morality reflects His holy character. Second, true morality is realized when the standard of moral conduct is carried out voluntarily by the individual. This happens after the transition from external to internal authority takes place and the child begins to regulate his behavior from within.

A Case for Empathy

In *Growing Kids God's Way,* we stressed the importance of teaching your children godly values and virtues. After all, if there are no heavenly values to stir the heart, the heart will not be stirred toward righteousness. Children must learn what is right and what is wrong, and as soon as they are old enough they must understand why it is so.

The difference between knowing how to do right and knowing the why of doing right is central to our message. Knowing how to behave represents moral action; knowing why to behave represents moral principle. Many children know how to apply moral law. They have been taught what to do and what not to do, but not many know the moral reason why. Without the why there can be no empathy.

Empathy is a moral emotion that sooner or later becomes the barometer of moral maturity. Empathy is the ability to enter into another's emotions or feelings and, when appropriate, to act on those feelings.

We believe that children who lag behind in moral reasoning also lag behind in the virtue of rightly focused empathy. When a child is only trained to the letter of the law and not to the principle that the law represents, or when a child is trained solely how to do right or avoid wrong and not trained in the moral reason why, then the child is hindered in his ability to express empathy.

Returning to chapter one of *GKGW* can help clarify this point. In one portion of "How to Raise a Moral Child," young Ryan was instructed by his father to keep his light off and to stay on his bunk. When Ryan's younger brother fell out of bed, Ryan got up, turned on the light, and comforted his brother. Ryan understood his father's instruction and the context and purpose for which it was given. But he also knew it was not his father's intent to keep him in bed under all circumstances. Ryan responded with empathy.

He could have obeyed the letter of the law and stayed in bed, but to do so would have compromised the greater need of the moment – comforting his younger brother. Not only would the greater good be compromised, but his failure to provide comfort would have created a greater wrong.

You must move your preteen beyond external obedience. You must move him from:
1. The externalization of truth to
2. the internalization of truth to
3. the transfer of truth with *empathy.*

Or move your child from the:
1. Outward compliance to the letter of the law to
2. inward understanding of the principle behind the law to
3. taking action based on *empathy.*

The following illustration will further demonstrate these principles. Dave and Kim had not seen Larry and Sue since their ministry years back in Nebraska. For that evening's dessert, Kim baked Larry's favorite cake, topping it with a special maple frosting. Placing the cake on the kitchen table, she turned to ten-year-old Nate and said, "No finger swiping the edge of the frosting. In fact, do not touch the cake. It is a surprise dessert for Mr. Miller. I'm going next door and will be back in a half hour."

Kim left the kitchen while Nate continued working on his puzzle. A few minutes later Nate began to notice the angle of the sun changing and hot rays began to stream in through the window falling on the cake. He also realized that if the cake was not moved, the frosting would melt and ruin the dessert.

At this point Nate was confronted with a moral decision. The letter of the law said, "Do not touch the cake, it is a surprise dessert for Mr. Miller." But the intent of the law was also made known. "It's a surprise dessert for Mr. Miller." Because the intent was part of the instructions, Nate acted on it. He considered his mother's statement, but he also considered what she really meant. She meant that he was not to sample any part of the cake. Understanding the principle is what led him to act with empathy.

Nate took ownership of his mom's feelings. He understood her desire to do something special for the Millers. He knew how disappointed she would be if the cake were ruined because of a simple oversight and his lack of action. The principle of empathy was at work in Nate's heart. He was trained to look beyond the law to the greater principle. He took ownership of his mom's feelings and acted on them by moving the cake out of the sun's rays.

He could have done nothing, like Ryan laying in bed, and still have met the letter of the law. But like Ryan, he went beyond and did that which was morally superior – he acted with empathy.

Here is yet a third illustration. Ten-year-old Ryan supervised his younger brothers and their school friends in an informal soccer game, while the parents attended a teacher's meeting. Jill came with her parents directly from a wedding, so she had no play clothes. She stood on the side line with her white dress and shiny black shoes and watched the other kids play. Ryan, realizing that his classmate could not join because of her clothing, called the other kids over and started playing something that Jill could participate in. That was an empathy response. Ryan considered Jill, her feelings of non-involvement, the circumstances that prevented her participation, and then acted on it. Would your child do that? Does your child have the moral knowledge and convictions to do the same?

Approving That Which Is Excellent

The apostle Paul told the Philippian church to approve that which is excellent (Philippians 1:10a). The word *approve* means to test the way of excellence, to know what is genuine. The word *excellence* means over and above, beyond what is required.

GKGW parents do an excellent job of bringing their children to a minimum standard of moral compliance. They trained their children to respond appropriately when receiving a compliment or an acknowledgment from an adult. They know how to meet the external law. In the early years, such moral compliance is a duty thrust on the child by morally-sensitive parents. It is a moral obligation that you insist upon. But there must come a time when your child goes beyond the minimum requirement and *does the way of excellence*. This will truly demonstrate what is in your child's heart.

While getting out of our car, we met eight-year-old Timarie. She was standing on the sidewalk waiting for our arrival and subsequent visit with her parents. We made eye contact and said, "Hello. Are you one of the Smith children?" "Yes," she responded. Then she walked toward us with an adult-like confidence and put out her hand to shake ours. As she graciously met us with her eyes, she said with all sincerity, "Hello Mr. and Mrs. Ezzo. It is very nice to meet you. How was your trip over to Tucson?"

Impressed with the child's genuine interest in us, we asked the mother how she brought Timarie to this level of moral courtesy. Here is a summary of her thoughts.

In *Growing Kids God's Way*, we learned the progressive nature of *good, better,* and *best* and attempted to pass it on to our children. We explained to our kids that *good* represents them. It represents the minimum required in a moral situation. If someone says, "Hi," or extends a courtesy, the kind thing to do is to give back a "hi" or a "thank you."

Better represents our family. We encourage our children to take the next step in extending a courtesy. For example, when being introduced to an adult, we encouraged and showed our children how to graciously extend their hand and shake hands with the person they're meeting. Also, we stressed that shaking hands with your eyes is as important as shaking with your hands. Or, when sitting and a visitor walks into the room, they are to stand and acknowledge their presence. Such a gesture is based on 1 Corinthians 13:5, *love is not rude.*

Best, we taught our kids, represents God. It is doing over and above what is required. We want our children to know that while good may be acceptable, and better preferable, seeking to please God is

most desirable. So when Timarie extended her hand, and invited conversation by asking about your welfare, she was extending a courtesy the best way she knew how.

Proverbs 20:11, says, *Even a child is known by his deeds, whether what he does is pure and right.* A child's moral disposition will show itself, just as the new bud leads to a blossom and the blossom to the fruit. What is in your child's heart will blossom some day. A truth-loving, gracious child – how joyous is the prospect of the blossom and the fruit from this hopeful budding! Timarie's moral disposition showed itself with right principles – right principles placed there by her parents.

Take your middle years children to the next level of moral sensitivity. Go beyond good and better. Encourage them to strive for best – the excellence found in Christ.

HORMONES AND BODY CHANGES

Blaming hormones as the catalyst for teenage rebellion is popularly accepted throughout our society. Are the defiant acts and rebellious mood swings we witness set in motion by forces of nature at the onset of puberty? Is that when hormone demons take control of a teen's body?

Actually, hormonal changes in the endocrine system begin in children at about age seven, not twelve, which is commonly believed. Yes, your middle years child is hormonally active.

This new growth period marks the end of a hormonal suppression set in place soon after birth, and the beginning of many years of glandular arousal. At age seven the gonado-trophin hormone levels begin to rise in both boys and girls. The results are more readily apparent in girls. Have you ever wondered why your nine-year-old daughter can, in a cyclical way, change moods overnight, sometimes becoming emotionally irrational? She may go through cycles of discouragement, breaking out in sobbing tears over minor details. She spells a word wrong on her English report and cries out, "I can't do this!" She is now convinced she will never make it in school. Her face becomes a little more oily and she is sure everyone is noticing. For a few days she becomes more snippety toward her siblings.

Hormones and Body Changes

Surely physical growth (or lack of same) can add stress to a teen's life. However, while changes in the endocrine system may result in new patterns of behavior, glands don't affect attitudes of the heart. At the onset of puberty, for example, both boys and girls begin to change their minds about the opposite sex and start, all of a sudden, to view the other gender as being attractive. So now more attention is paid to personal hygiene and grooming, with a heightened sensitivity to appearances and dress.

This is why physical characteristics, which mark the individual as different from his peers, may constitute a source of personal anxiety and stress. We know that disproportionate and uneven body growth, clumsiness, unhealthy complexion due to skin blemishes, and feelings of inadequacy for not measuring up to the ideal all play a part in how a teen views himself and his world.

Body Changes and Emotions

There is no question that during the later preteen and teen years emotions become more complex. In pubescent girls, disturbances in homeostasis can be experienced. For several days preceding and during their menstrual cycles, hormonal imbalances affect blood pressure, body temperature, basal metabolism, and water accumulation (which may press on nerve centers). These factors may lead to tension, irritability, and general nervousness.

An excess or gross deficiency of one or more of the hormones produced by the glands of the endocrine system can also affect personality. A hyperthyroid condition, for example, can make a child nervous, excited, jumpy, restless, and overactive. A hypothyroid condition causes children to be lethargic, unresponsive, dissatisfied, even depressed. But these are the exceptions, not the norm. This may explain poor behavior, but it does not legitimize it.

Hormones' Indirect Effects

Hormones may affect personality but not morality. The theoretical link between hormones and changes in teen behavior is measurable, but to link hormone levels and teenage rebellion is a stretch. Glandular surges do not cause children to lie, steal, cheat, act disrespectfully, or to relationally wander away from their parents. In a nutshell, hormones may affect the human body, but not the human heart.

Hormones may exacerbate already weak relationships, but they don't create them, as suggested by modern theory. At worst, hormones have an *indirect* effect on relationships.

For example, your twelve-year-old son starts to pay more attention to grooming and his appearance in public because of his attraction to the opposite sex. Trouble brews when his peers' choices in music and hair style conflict with your preferences, or when he wants to go out and meet the gang and you want him to stay home and finish his school project. The battle begins, and back and forth you go. Please note, though, that the problem is rooted in values, not an increase in testosterone.

A fifteen-year-old girl retains fluids during her menses and feels bloated. Becoming dissatisfied with her appearance, she pushes herself into a semi-starvation pattern of eating. Her parents forbid this type of dietary behavior, insisting that she eat balanced meals. Relational tension builds up, and daily arguments ensue. The daughter declares, "You don't understand!" "You don't love me!" In this scenario and hundreds like it, only the names of the participants change. Again, please note: It is not hormones or puberty that cause stress, but it is the relationship. The daughter's wrong view of herself and the inappropriate way she dealt with it set the problem in motion. No hormone demon sat upon her shoulder and shouted "Ugly, ugly, ugly."

Here are some basic facts to consider: If hormones cause rebellion, the phenomenon would be universal and measurable in all societies and cultures. The genetic time clock would kick in for all children, bringing about rebellion in all adolescents. But it doesn't. Not in any culture does this universally happen, including ours.

What about teens who come out of healthy families? They go through the same hormonal changes but do not rebel. And if hormones were the sole culprit and cause of adolescent defiance, then medication could easily treat the condition.

Do hormones influence behavior? Of course they do. But we ask the reader to neither minimize nor elevate their influence but to understand them. Hormones do play a significant role in influencing behavior – just not as dominant a one as our society suggests.

Questions for Review

1. In the Christian home, moral adherence is dependent on what three factors?

2. What are the two components of true morality?

3. What is empathy?

4. Explain the moral levels of good, better, and best.

5. Explain the following statement: "Hormones may affect the human body but not the heart."

6

The Power of Groupthink

Although socializing with age-peers is a natural part of growing up, it's not until the middle and early teen years that a child becomes fully aware of what it means to belong to a group of peers. Actually, it is not until this time that parents really begin to understand the full impact of peer relationships.

A peer culture constitutes a growing influence on how an adolescent thinks and acts because the family is no longer the single influencing voice on the child. And while teachers, coaches, and Sunday school workers all have an influence, none shape behavior with the greatest of ease as does an age-related peer.

The middle years is a time when a child moves from an awakening to a full awareness of the significance of the group's opinion. That is what brings about age-related peer pressure. The child from a distance wants to know, "What does the group think?" Closer up, he wants to know, "What does the group think of me?"

It is a natural tendency to seek social approval. We all feel satisfied to be a part of a group. The same is true with our children. Conforming to the peer group standards and expectations facilitates a preteen's and teen's sense of social belonging and standing. And

consequently, a child learns early on that any deviation from the standards of the group could mean nonacceptance, ridicule, and even rejection. Thus, peer pressure finds its genesis in the need to conform.

PEER PRESSURE

What is peer pressure? Peer pressure is a socializing force that continually challenges the status quo of one's thinking and behavior. Peer pressure on children is not always negative and does not become so unless the peer-culture's values stand in opposition to those of the parents. Complications arise when the standards established in the home strongly conflict with those of other parents and children in the community.

To ensure peer acceptance under such conditions, the teen learns that he must accept the group's interests and values. He cannot afford to be different because this would jeopardize his status within the group. To demonstrate his allegiance, he acts out his new association and conforms to the group's identity. This might be represented by choices in hairstyle, clothes, music, and the use of slang or foul language.

The teen must assess and decide what is more significant: the approval of his peers or the approval of his parents – or find for himself a happy medium. Unfortunately, that usually means one set of rules to satisfy the peers and another set to satisfy Mom and Dad. This double life is really a double lie only leading to conflict and an increase in oppositional pressure to conform to both parents and peers.

COMBATTING NEGATIVE PEER PRESSURE

It isn't the power of peer pressure that tears adolescents from their parents but a conflict in values that makes teens more vulnerable to peer pressure. The closer the values between parents and teen, the stronger the allegiance and the less likely that the teen will drift away from the parents. Please understand that the healthy *GKGW* family does not eliminate normal peer pressure as much as it develops healthy ways to deal with it. This is why it is wrong to blame peer pressure as the primary cause of drug use, crime, rebellion, sexual promiscuity, and the general breakdown of the family. Fundamentally, the problem is a matter of incompatible values.

There are some things you need to do to protect your children from negative peer pressure while reinforcing your values. Take advantage of:

1. The power of sanctifying grace.
2. The power of family identity.
3. The power of community.

The Power of Sanctifying Grace

The duty of Christian parents to instruct their children in the knowledge of God cannot be achieved apart from His grace. The ultimate issue in parenting is the salvation of the child, and it is true that salvation is by grace alone, through faith alone (Eph. 2:8-9). Yet, many parents wrongly conclude that dependency upon grace means that they should "let go and let God." But how can parents expect the communication of grace unless we "wait upon God" in the manner prescribed in Scripture? Such "waiting" does not lead to passivity but rather to an understanding that God's grace is applied through our labor (Col. 1:29).

In his essays on the duties of a parent, the nineteenth century English cleric John C. Ryle warned parents to beware of that miserable delusion into which some have fallen – namely, that parents can do nothing for their children but must leave them alone, wait for grace, and sit still. Pastor Ryle understood well the importance of early training and passionately exhorted parents to participate in the communication of God's grace by opening the child's mind and directing his ways in God's moral law. For in so doing, children are brought to a servant-knowledge of God. The "passive parenting" model is subtly attractive because its emphasis on grace has the appearance of biblical piety. Yet, it fails to place an equal emphasis on the truth that God at times administers His grace through the labors of Christian parents.

Of the various means by which God communicates His grace, three deserve our attention here. First, there is a *common grace* given to all people – the benefits of which are experienced by the whole human race without discrimination. For instance, God brings refreshing rain on the righteous and the unrighteous alike.

Second, there is *sanctifying grace*. God's grace flows to families through the sanctifying grace of believing spouses and parents. But to obtain for our children the spiritual and saving blessings comprised in the gracious promises of God's Word, we (the governors of their souls) must believe and be faithfully obedient to God's revelation. Without faith, we have no title to any blessings of promise.

Without obedience, we cannot expect the favor of God and the communication of His grace on our children or on our efforts. Grace is communicated to each household, as long as parents stay vertically aligned with the Lord.

A third medium is *regenerational grace.* How basic this truth is to our entire *Growing Kids God's Way* and *Middle Years* presentation! No morality or conformity to the moral law can be acceptable to God, except that which is exercised in total dependence on Jesus Christ from a heart secured by Him. God delights in right behavior which arises from a right heart. Apart from receiving a new heart from the regenerating work of the Holy Spirit, no child has direct and personal access to God's grace.

Does this negate the divine call for parents to "train up a child in the way of the Lord"? Most certainly not. It only serves to energize even more the parents' need to cooperate with the grace of God. A biblical view of grace doesn't mean parents labor less; rather, they labor fervently, all the while acknowledging their utter dependency upon God. Such parents will be known as people of the Word and people of prayer.

Seek diligently the salvation of your child that they might enter the fullness of God's power and influence and out of a love response to God serve Him wholeheartedly. In parenting, grace and labor are not enemies but divinely appointed comrades in the work of the Lord. You cannot parent by your own strength and still achieve a godly outcome. Remember to let God through His grace do His part, while you through obedience do yours.

The Power of Family Identity

Do not underestimate the power of your family identity. Identity association is a visible life-on-life dynamic found in all human relationships. It is a socializing process by which a person identifies himself with a group he is familiar with, attracted to, or feels empathy with. We derive from our identity associations our sense of belonging, and we give back to these associations varying degrees of allegiance.

Among behavioral scientists, it is commonly accepted that teens are driven by a natural quest to find their own identity, and that they use peers to help establish and then validate what they believe. However, that's not true of teens who are members of an *interdependent* family – that is, where family members are mutually dependent upon each other. Within the comfortable confines of the interdependent family, parents, not peers, usually have the greater influence.

The very nature of progressive development reveals that teens choose their community identity (that is, their peer friends) only after their family identity is: 1) established, and 2) accepted or rejected. If the family is accepted as the primary source of values and comfort, then the teen not only identifies with home, but makes friends from among those possessing similar values. This creates positive peer pressure. When there is harmony between the core beliefs of parents and teens, both seek similar values in other families and friends. That is why, ultimately:

Peer pressure on a child is only as strong as family identity is weak.

The closer the values between parents and teen, the stronger the allegiance and the less likely that the teen will drift away from the parents. Values-based parenting wonderfully facilitates the natural process by which children first associate with their parents, then gain a sense of belonging, and finally pledge their allegiance to the family.

In healthy families, adolescence is not a time when teens seek a new identity but rather attempt to validate the one they already have. Any identity crisis for these kids took place at age two, not at fifteen.

Unless driven away by unmet relational needs, teens don't seek a primary identity apart from their families. Unlike what some seem to want us to believe, there is no hidden, genetically controlled, instinctive dynamic whereby teens automatically reject their parents and family in favor of peers – and that's good news for family relationships.

The Power of Community

As family educators and as parents, we believe strongly in family identity. But even family identity is not sufficient to carry you through the preteen years. You need something more – something bigger than your family. You need the power of community.

The word *community* can mean many things to many people. We use it to refer to a society of families, tied together, sharing common interests, values, and a significant commitment to an ideal, for the mutual benefit of the individual and the collective membership. In other words, to quote the Three Musketeers, "All for one and one for all!"

Why is it important to have a community? Because a community does something that nothing else can; it establishes within the group a sense of "we-ness" that encourages members to work toward a common good, guided by common values.

Since members of your community are going to teach your children (directly or indirectly), it is vital that you surround yourself with people who share your morals and your values. In a moral community, you will find people who, like you, are striving to live out the biblical precepts of respect and honor and instill in their children a biblical awareness and consideration of others. These are the kind of people who can provide a support group for you, Mom and Dad.

Another reason you need a like-minded, moral community is that within your community (whatever that community may be) your child will find other kids to spend time with. You want those to be healthy, moral kids – kids whose moms and dads are working to instill biblical values in their hearts just as you are with your child.

In the years ahead, broader interests and attachment to friends will become more meaningful to your son or daughter. In the truest sense, he or she is becoming morally and relationally emancipated and self-reliant. That is why the moral community in which you and your child belong will either be a friend or foe to your family values.

The greater the disparity between the values of your family and your family community (from which you and your child will both draw your peers), the greater will be the source of conflict within the home. The opposite of this is also true; shared values between community and home result in positive peer pressure on your child.

For example, if a teen had a negligent parent during the 1950s, neighbors, teachers, little league coaches, and the community at large provided the moral direction the child was lacking. This happened because communities operated from one set of values. All values had common meaning; nothing was relative. Today, we live in a society that believes that *values* and *virtues* are relative. As a result, common moral communities are virtually nonexistent. That is why today you can be a good parent and still turn out a wayward child.

Being immersed in a moral community is absolutely necessary if you hope to have your values reinforced. When your child's peers come out of a like-minded community, he or she will be reassured of the importance of family values. Furthermore, confidence in you, Mom and Dad, is strengthened. Once your child finds friends in your moral community, those friends become a source of positive peer pressure and healthy groupthink.

This truth is illustrated by the story of a young girl we know whose orthodontist decided that she needed to wear headgear. Though he strongly recommended that she wear the headgear twenty-four hours a day, he said to her with the greatest sensitivity, "I realize, though, that you probably can't wear it at school because the kids might laugh at you."

"Oh, no," the girl told him. "Not at my school. The kids won't laugh at me there." This child felt secure in her community. She knew she would not be ridiculed. This gave her the strength she needed to help her do what she knew was best – wear the headgear at all times.

How would your child respond in this situation? Would the children in his or her circle of friends say, "Do what's right. Wear the headgear"? Or would they say, "Don't listen to your mom and dad. You look like a dork"? It is time to take a look at who is in your family's community.

At this point, we must make one important clarification. By stating that you must surround your family with people who share your morals and values, we are not saying that you should isolate your children from the world. Nothing could be further from the truth. To isolate yourself into a moral community is as unbiblical as it is to say that you don't need a moral community to help you raise your children. No, parents should not isolate children from nonbelievers. Jesus calls us to be salt and light to the world (Matthew 5:13-14). However, we do want to insulate our children from corruptive influences.

When our family lived in New England years ago, every floor, ceiling, and outside wall was insulated. As parents, we insulated our home because we did not want the elements to disturb the healthy environment we were providing for our children. That insulation did not keep every element out. Yes, it slowed the process of cold coming into our house, but it did not keep the wind from rushing in when the door was opened. It was also true that we could not stay in the house all the time. It was necessary and important for us to go out into the world around us. The insulated house did, however, give us a place where we could find safety and warmth.

By the same token, a moral community insulates your child against the elements of the world. Through association with like-minded peers, our children see family standards reinforced by others who share the same values. The strength they draw from moral peers is the very thing that makes it possible for Mom and Dad to let them participate in city Little League or a community soccer league. The support of a moral community allows our families to go and minister, knowing that the moral strength drawn from our like-minded community allows us to present something very beautiful to the world.

SUMMARY

The middle years is a time of change. It is the last phase of immaturity and the transition to moral maturity. Moral maturity is characterized by an increased capacity to direct one's own behavior by intrinsic values, to judge adequately right from wrong, and to know why it is so. The middle years is also the time when gradual physiological changes begin to nudge children to a new awareness of themselves and that of the opposite sex. This spawns a new era of significant peer relationships. New social stresses are placed on the child, and as a result, the parent-child relationship. Yet, this has always been so and will continue as long as people live on this earth. God knew that and He did not leave us hopeless or helpless. Parents do make the difference when it comes to healthy parent-teen relationships because parents make choices every day. How obedient are you to God – every day? Have you been working on your family identity – every day? Who is in your community of friends – every day? These are just a few of the questions that need an honest evaluation because the consequences to these questions can make all the difference in the world as to how your family turns out.

Questions for Review

1. When does peer pressure become negative?

2. What makes teens more vulnerable to peer pressure?

3. Define and explain identity association.

4. Explain why negligent parents could still raise good children fifty years ago, and why good parents can raise a wayward child today.

5. Explain why community is important to the successful rearing of children.

7

Communication and Conversation

Communication is an important part of relationships. Speaking and listening are God-given abilities that enable us to verbally express feelings, utter sound with meaning, and write words with intent. God understands our need for communication. He Himself is a communicating and conversational God. The Bible abounds with examples of this. The Lord spoke to Adam and Eve in the garden, the child Samuel in the temple, Moses from a burning bush, and the list continues with hundreds of uses of the phrase, "The Lord said."

Not only does God speak, but He listens. He listens to the cries of His people and hears their prayers. He's not only the creator of communication but the supreme example of its use. In contrast, we can all improve our skills. We can listen more attentively and speak more graciously. But communication skills cannot make up for a lack of relational health. Communication has become a catch-word in discussions about troubled marriages and struggling parents. While a lack of communication usually is a symptom of an unhealthy relationship, it is not necessarily true that poor communication was the cause of it. Being skilled in communication techniques does not guarantee family harmony or healthy relation-

ships. Communication skills are not a substitute for values. What holds families together is the moral unity found within the soul of the family. Moral intimacy among family members has no substitute, no backup, no replacement. That's why we believe *good speaking and listening skills are important parts of healthy relationships but are not a substitute for them.*

We probably all know of great communicators who have little if any relationship with their kids. And even worse, they may have kids who desire no relationship with them. This only proves our point that good communication skills are not a substitute for good values. Knowing how to communicate with your spouse and kids is certainly important, but even more important is first learning how to biblically love and live with your family. Unconditional love not only should be the basis of our communication; it is the ultimate medium for developing the rapport that characterizes healthy families.

In this chapter, we will address the factors that influence healthy preteen and teen communication. It starts with the ethics governing how we speak and listen.

THE ETHICS OF COMMUNICATION

Creating and maintaining a climate of trust

where our kids feel secure enough to openly and honestly communicate with us continues to be a high priority for parents of preteens. Success in this endeavor requires that we submit ourselves to the ethics of Scripture governing how we speak and listen. For example, Proverbs 15:1 speaks of the tone of our words: "A soft answer turns away wrath, but harsh words stir up anger." Proverbs 16:21 describes the influence of our words: "The wise in heart will be called prudent, and sweetness of the lips increases learning." In Proverbs 25:11 we learn of the importance of a timely message: "A word fitly spoken is like apples of gold," and again in verse 20, "Like one who takes away a garment in cold weather and like vinegar on soda, is one who sings songs to a heavy heart."

Proverbs 16:24 speaks of the care we should take in selecting positive words: "Pleasant words are like a honeycomb. Sweetness to the soul and health to the bones." And somewhat similar, Colossians 4:6 encourages us to employ well-chosen words: "Let your speech always be with grace, seasoned with salt, that you may know how you ought to answer each one."

The ethics of Scripture also govern listening. Proverbs 18:13 instructs us to listen to all facets of an issue before speaking: "He who answers a matter before he hears it, it is folly and shame to him." Proverbs 18:17 teaches us not to listen to just one side of the story: "The first one to plead his cause seems right. Until his neighbor comes and examines him." Proverbs 1:33 charges us to listen to the voice of wisdom for our own safety: "But whosoever listens to me will dwell safely, and will be secure, without fear of evil." And finally, we have these words of wisdom from the book of James: "Let everyone be quick to hear, slow to speak," *and as a result,* "slow to anger" (James 1:19). We actually esteem others

higher, fulfilling the biblical admonishment of Philippians 2:3, when we pay attention to the two components of speaking and listening.

INFLUENCES ON HEALTHY PRETEEN AND TEEN COMMUNICATION

Healthy, proactive communication is one of the best forms of preteen and adolescent encouragement. Good communication can prevent more conflicts than corrections can solve. Teens communicate their feelings much more readily than younger children, possibly because their vocabulary is more mature and the words needed to reflect inner abstract feelings are now present. Whatever the reason, meaningful talk can take place during adolescence, so take advantage of this opportunity. Learn how to talk so your kids will listen, and learn to listen so your kids will talk.

Healthy communication serves as a vehicle to transfer our thoughts, emotions, feelings, and ideas. We must work to perfect the communication skills that bring legitimacy to our words and willingness on the part of our preteens to listen to us. Below are seven suggestions to help improve your parent-preteen communication.

Different Genders, Different Needs

A number of years ago, my mentor Dr. Fred Barshaw gave me some insights when it comes to communicating with sons. I needed his insights. He had sons and no daughters and we had daughters and no sons. His insights have proven to be helpful ever since. This is what he taught me.

When attempting to correct a situation through communication, adolescent boys tend to feel more comfortable with *indirect* conversation. That is, instead of sitting down face to face, go outside and work on the fence, tune up the car, or go to the workshop and finish painting the screens. When working on a common task together, sons tend to listen without feeling threatened and tend to commit themselves to change more readily than if you sat on a couch, face to face and talked through an issue.

Adolescent girls are just the opposite. They tend to feel more comfortable with direct conversation. That is, they seek face to face, heart to heart dialogue. In fact, if Mom said, "Here is the dish towel. You dry, I'll wash, and we'll talk about your troubling attitude toward your brother," the daughter would be less receptive than if they both sat together and talked face to face.

Remember these handy truths. Adolescent girls like direct focusing attention, adolescent boys tend to respond better to parental criticism by the indirect method. Getting the point across is the goal, not conforming your child to a method.

Creating Opportunity to Talk

The primary times of talking in the Ezzo household were at dinner and bedtime. When our kids started through the middle years, we talked more at dinner than at bedtime. But when they began to hit the teens years, we talked more at bedtime than at any other time. We had an interesting arrangement. Some nights the girls sat on the edge of our bed, tucking their mother and me in while recounting the day's activities. The next night it was our turn to sit on the edge of their beds and talk.

Our nightly efforts accomplished more than simply providing an extended time to talk. They provided a necessary opportunity to care for our family at a deeper level of communion. All those nights spent sitting on each other's beds, listening to one another, and participating in meaningful conversation ministered to each of us at a deeper level than could be achieved at most other times.

We would interact with each other and try to empathize with what each one said or thought. We connected to each other at a deeper level than was possible with the conversation we might expect to have at other times when we would talk about Dad's day at work or the kid's day at school.

This was a powerful experience. The deep impression of "the family" residing in each member's heart united us in ways that no principle alone can explain. Just as our communion with Jesus Christ is not merely appreciation for the ink and type on the pages of the Bible but is instead a deep and abiding relationship such as that of the Father with His Son – "As you Father are in me and I in you" (John 17:21a), so also is this dynamic expressed as the talking soul of the family. When talktime didn't take place for one reason or another, there was much discontent and loneliness among our family members.

Some families don't know what they don't have. They don't realize the value of time – of using their special moments to develop the soul of the family – until they no longer have it.

Listen for Content and Intent

In the 1970s, comedian Flip Wilson popularized the cliché, "Read my lips." Parents need to do more than read their kids' lips; they need to read their hearts. Healthy communication requires that parents listen to what is being felt as much as what is actually being said. Try to understand the message of your teen's heart. Not to do so, in effect, rejects your child. We play a dangerous and destructive game if we routinely fail to listen to feelings.

On one occasion, our daughter Amy shared that she had no close friends. I responded off the cuff, "Of course you do. Don't be silly!" Although I was trying to sound encouraging, I actually cut her communication short. I listened to her words but not to her feelings. Later that evening, Anne Marie informed me of a struggle Amy was having with a close friend. In this case, she had responded by listening to the deeper message – listening between the lines rather than reacting only to the words on the surface.

When listening for the unspoken message being communicated, concentrate on the way your son or daughter is speaking – the body language, facial expression, tone of voice, and sense of urgency. Parents gain greater insights, knowledge, and sensitivity when they listen to non-verbal messages.

The benefits are enormous because preteens and teens respond positively and grow in their confidence that you care about what they feel and think. In-depth listening gives your children the respect they deserve and sets the standard of respect and focused attention that you require from them when it is your turn to talk.

Provide for a "ten-talk"

"Dad, I need to talk with you, and this is a ten-talk." One of the great hindrances to relational communication is time availability. Sometimes we just can't stop and talk and give our full attention when our children ask for it. Sometimes our kids want to talk, just to talk, and sometimes they need to talk – right now.

How do you find the right balance between meeting their immediate needs and staying focused on the project in front of you, which may equally need your attention? To find that balance in our family, we used the ten-talk rule. It was a privilege and a sacred trust to invoke this rule. If our children absolutely and imme-

diately needed our attention, they could have it by telling us they needed a ten-talk. Based on a scale of one to ten, ten being most urgent, our children were trusted to grade their own need and tell us. The grading between one and five represents, "I want to talk with you," and between six and ten means, "I need to talk with you." Here, in more detail, is how the grading system worked in our family.

Ten-Talk means: "This is most urgent; I need to talk right now, Dad."

Eight-Talk means: "This is urgent. Can you give me some time in the next hour?"

Six-Talk means: "As soon as you're done, Dad, we need to talk. Even if it means later tonight."

Four-Talk means: "Dad, when you find some time for me today, tonight, or tomorrow, I would like to talk with you."

Two-Talk means: "Dad, get back to me sometime. I have some questions to ask you."

As mentioned, our ten-talk rule was a privilege, and it was taken seriously. It meant we were going to trust our children to assess the urgency of their need in light of our present activities. Obviously, my time availability when sitting in deep concentration in front of my computer while working on a message is less flexible than when sitting in a chair reading a Louis L'Amour western.

Before coming into my office and evoking an eight- or ten-talk rule, my children gave plenty of thought to what they were asking. Could it wait a few minutes, hours, or even days? Could Mom answer the question? Our kids knew we trusted them with the privilege of their own assessment. They knew also that we could be trusted to listen attentively and completely when they really needed it. That mutual trust further served to build our healthy communication.

Guard Your Tongue and Your Tone

A useful adaptation of the old proverb, "Think before you speak" is: guard your tongue and your tone and learn to measure your thoughts against your teen's excitement. I had to learn this myself. I'm the type of person who does not like radical change, especially if there is no warning. So you can imagine the scene in our home some years ago when my teenage daughters waltzed into the room with new hair perms, eagerly seeking Dad's blessing on their endeavor. With their hands bouncing tightly coiled new curls (where, from my perspective, there had recently been beautiful straight hair) and glancing first at me, then toward the mirror, they asked hopefully, "Dad, how do you like it?" I stared, allowing my senses to take it all in. Then I said something dumb like, "Does your mother know you did that?"

Once uttered, those words could not be called back. Nor could I return to two pretty faces the hope that Dad, the most important man in their lives, would share in their fun and excitement of the moment. My tongue and tone robbed their hearts of the joy of sharing their excitement. I learned from that experience, and others like it, to gauge my responses against the excitement on their faces.

I also learned something about myself. In two days I always seemed to end up liking the changes anyway. I actually was a little disappointed when they went back to wearing straight hair!

As parents we sometimes make rash statements without thinking of the potential con-sequences of our words. Building a trusting, loving, and respectful relationship with our kids during the vulnerable middle years requires emotional gentleness. Guard your tongue and your tone and measure your responses against the excitement on your children's faces. Do this before they decide you are not one to be trusted with the joys of their lives.

Must Talk and Listen with Empathy

One day our daughter came home from high school. From the look on her face to the droop of her shoulders, I knew something was wrong. I risked an exploratory statement. "Jen, you look like you're hurting. It's obvious that it hasn't been a good day. I'm sorry about that." She looked at me with a halfhearted smile, "It's nothing, Dad."

I decided not to pry. I remembered on more than one occasion when a person's, "Do you want to talk about it?" put me off. Sometimes we need to pick with whom and when we share troubles. My statement let her know that I cared; the rest was up to her.

Later that afternoon, I was weeding my garden when Jenny came outside, pulled up a crate, and sat down. She started sharing about Martha, a new girl she had befriended. It seemed that Martha had also become friends with Jenny's best friend, Sarah. Suddenly, Jenny was no longer included in Martha and Sarah's plans. She had been nudged out and made a third wheel. It hurt.

Jennifer asked, "Why, Dad, after all these years of being best friends, would Sarah just drop me like that? Sarah wears Martha's clothes and her jewelry and goes home with her after school. And she has only known her for a couple of weeks if that long? It doesn't make sense."

"It hurts when that happens," I said, "watching your best friend take off with the new kid, especially the kid you introduced her to." Jenny reacted curiously to that statement. It never occurred to her that one of her parents might have lost a best friend in a similar manner. I began to reflect on an incident from my own youth.

Afterward Jenny asked, "What do you think I should do?" "Wait, I guess. Give it some time. Don't try to force yourself into the relationship by playing the same game Martha did. That will only rob you of your integrity. Be gracious with Sarah; maybe she will see that real friendships can never be bought with fancy clothes and expensive jewelry. If you and Sarah were really best friends, she'll come back. Real friendships are not forgotten."

For a teen struggling with life, there is no more important resource than a parent with a capacity for empathy. Letting our kids know that we understand what they are feeling because we have been there ourselves serves to tighten the relational ties. It is a concrete way for them to know we truly do understand.

Incidentally, one day a week later, Jennifer came waltzing into my office after school. She wore a smile that lit up the room. She looked at me and with a twinkle in her eye said; "Dad, Sarah wrote me a note today and apologized for being such a jerk. She told me how foolish she had been to think that all of Martha's beautiful clothes and flashy jewelry could ever replace me. She wants us to be best friends like we always have been."

We hugged and Jenny whispered, "Thanks, Dad. You were right. I waited, and she came back."

We've lost track of how many times since then that Jenny and Amy have asked either of us, "Did you ever go through something like

this?" Empathy breeds confidence in parental counsel. Share yourself with your kids. Share your failures and your successes, your own adolescent hurts and pains. They need to know that you have been there emotionally.

Communicating Empathy Through Life Stories

The middle years is a transition and growing emotional complexity. Understandably, some children lack confidence and develop feelings of inadequacy when facing new situations. Sometimes they feel emotionally isolated because they think (just as you did when you were their age) that you, Mom and Dad, could never understand what he or she is going through. And yet we all know that is not true. Although it was a different time and place, the emotions we experienced in our youth were just as real as the ones our kids are living today. But do your kids know that?

No one reaches adulthood without the experience of betrayal, an unkind word, rejection, disappointment, grief, joy, unexpected pleasure, and triumph. Attached to every one of these emotions is a personal story, and our kids need to hear those stories. They need to know that we really do understand, and they need to know these things long before they experience these emotions themselves. Help equip your children to handle life through your own life stories.

There is something about sharing life stories with our kids that takes us beyond a mere desire for entertainment and distraction from the normal day. Stories often reflect our own emotional struggles, fears, pains, and sense for adventure. They also communicate the assurance that we are not emotionally isolated in this world. Others feel as we feel and know the good and bad times and feelings of pain or joy.

Even more powerful are the stories about

Mom and Dad and their childhood. We have already lived every emotion our children will experience. Each one of us can share stories of our past that reflect every emotion. Here is one from our past.

While baseball was the national pastime in the 1950s, as it is today, fishing was my sport. I loved to hit a stream or a lake for the day, and enjoyed myself more when I knew I could fish somewhere guaranteed to give me a day's catch. That is why I was excited to receive Mr. and Mrs. Wadsworth's invitation to join them the following weekend when they opened their cottage on White Birch Lake. It was the bluegill heaven – teeming with fish ready to hit anything offered as bait.

The Wadsworth's had high expectations of going and told my parents they would call early on Saturday morning to confirm it. If we did not get a call, then they would go some other time.

All week I waited with great anticipation of what the weekend would offer. On Friday night, I readied my equipment, dug my worms, checked my poles, and put out my boots. I was ready for what I had hoped to be a day of fishing. When 8:00 a.m. rolled around the next morning, the phone rang. I just knew it was Mr. Wadsworth. The voice on the other end told my mom, "Get the boy ready, we're going. We'll be by in ten minutes." "Okay," my mom said, "he'll be ready." I was going.

In less than two minutes I gathered my poles, worms, and tackle box, and dashed to the end of the driveway. There I stood, looking up the road, anticipating the Wadsworth's' silver, 1950 Plymouth heading my way. It was springtime, the sun was out, no school, and life was good.

I waited five, ten, and then fifteen minutes. I reminded myself about being patient. Older people in their forties are sometimes slow and forgetful. They probably just forgot a few things. They'll be coming – I'm sure of it.

But then I waited another twenty minutes and began to wonder if something had happened. The Wadworths only lived down the street.

I went into the house to ask my mom to call. Maybe there was some confusion. Maybe I was to meet them at their place. What if they were waiting for me? Worse I thought – what if they left without me? My mom dialed them up while I went back to the road side.

I found out later how the conversation went. "Henry, this is Anna Ezzo. Gary's been waiting for you out front, ever since you called. Will you be coming by shortly?" "Anna there must be a mistake," Henry said. "We never called you this morning. Something came up at the last minute, and we're not going up to the lake." It was then my mother realized the amazing coincidence. The first call was a wrong number. Whoever called just happened to say enough right things to make my mom think it was Mr. Wadsworth. In my minds eye I still can see my mother walking down the driveway toward me. I knew by looking on her face that I wasn't going fishing.

All the hopes that a little boy's imagination could muster were dashed. I had already borrowed from the anticipated excitement, only to have been let down by a wrong number. In that moment, I knew disappointment, and I was overwhelmed by it.

Disappointment. It's defined as the emotion felt when you experience something less than what you anticipated, were promised, or planned on. Yes, on that May morning in 1957, I knew disappointment.

But more importantly for the present, I

knew my children would face many disappointments in their growing up years and I wanted to make sure that they knew I understood disappointment. Your children need to know that you understand what each emotion feels like. Here's what we are suggesting to help you:

On a sheet of paper, list the most common human emotions you can think of. For example, list disappointment, joy, anger, feelings of victory, hurt, rejection, and others. Then think back to your own childhood. Every one of these emotions has a story with your name attached to it. After dinner or while on a walk, take an emotion and do a word study from the Bible. How did Old and New Testament characters deal with these emotions? Then share one of your stories with your kids.

Sharing life stories is more than entertaining; it is emotionally educational. You're depositing confidence into their memories by offering pieces of your life that they can presently relate to. The confidence gained from hearing about your life will keep them turning to you when their emotions are stretched and challenged.

Questions for Review

1. Of the ethics of Scripture, which ones do you feel parents most commonly violate? Which ones do you most often violate?

2. What does it mean to listen for content and intent?

3. What is the teen's responsibility before calling for a ten-talk?

4. What principle lies behind the suggestion to guard your tongue and your tone?

5. Why should you tell your children your life stories?

8

How To Encourage

When you encourage your preteen or teen in the context of a biblical relationship, you are offering a powerful motivator for right behavior and a strong incentive to become a moral teen. There are right ways to encourage and there are wrong ways. Let's look at both.

MOTIVATING WITH ENCOURAGEMENT

There are a number of ways to encourage your middle years child. Verbal praise, physical touch, simple gifts, spending time together, acts of service — each expression of love sends the message that we notice what our kids do, and that we care about them. But encouragement doesn't just happen. No matter which form of it we use, we must take the time to really notice behavior and then single out the positive aspects of it by relating it to the individual doing it. Encouragement requires parents to go the extra mile because it forces them to be relationally proactive.

In the above sentence, *relationally proactive* is a key concept because the dynamics associated with encouraging your middle years child are different from those involving your younger child. We encourage younger children out of the context of our authority and in order to bring about right behavior. We encourage our middle years children out of the context of our growing relationship and in response to our relationship. That is why a simple but common "Thank you, I appreciate your help," is more meaningful to a ten year old than it is to a three year old. Seven more years of relationship add greater meaning to such words of appreciation and praise. Here are some specific ways you can encourage your preteen and teen.

With Words

In healthy relationships, verbal affirmation is never redundant. Each of us enjoys receiving a pat on the back or hearing, "Well done," from someone we respect. We appreciate hearing how our actions pleased or helped another. Teens are no different. Like the rest of us, they are powerfully encouraged when justified praise comes their way.

If we are not verbalizing our encouragement, what message are we sending? Verbally encourage your teens in the little things and the big. It's easier to catch their big efforts, but many times it's the daily stuff that makes or breaks relationships. Sometimes a simple, "Thank you," can go a long way.

Another way to verbally encourage a child

is to say, "I need your help," instead of, "I want it," or just, "Do this." The humbleness it takes to ask for help – expressing sincere needs – elevates the other person.

If you are just getting started on the encouragement side of your relationship, be careful not to qualify your encouragement. Don't say, "Thanks for doing the dishes tonight. Miracles never cease." Or, "You prepared a great meal; too bad the potatoes are scorched." Such qualified encouragement is not encouragement at all.

With Touch

The touch of a gentle hand, a tender hug, or a pat on the back can all convey a message of encouragement. Physical encouragement communicates support, whether in victory or defeat. It fills in when words fail or aren't enough.

To hold and be held communicates vulnerability and a closeness that is reserved for trusting members of a family. For those with a struggling relationship with their preteens, this may mean starting slowly.

Simply placing a hand on the son's or daughter's shoulder and saying, "Great game," "Great job," or, "Thank you," may be appropriate. At other times, a high-five or a hug may be best. Whatever the case, don't underestimate the powerful influence of physical encouragement on your middle years son or daughter.

Anne Marie was always great at combining words of encouragement and simple but meaningful expressions of physical touch. Sometimes she would just stop the kids, put her hands on their shoulders, and with great sincerity say, "I just want you to know how much I appreciate the way you…" Verbal affirmation combined with physical touch are an unbeatable combination.

There is a tendency to use the encouragement of touch only when we're happy. But if we have had a bad day, believe me, our preteens and teens will notice if we put a gentle hand on their shoulder to say so. Consciously or unconsciously, they will appreciate the added effort and emotional cost the gesture took.

Gift-Giving

Preteens and teens relish being appreciated. One way to show this is through gift-giving. Giving a gift in response to a child's act of loving service is a great way to remind the child that you have not forgotten what he or she did.

We have tried to practice spontaneous gift-giving in our home. There were occasions when Anne Marie and I rushed out to a meeting, leaving the kitchen in disarray. Coming home to a spotless kitchen without having prompted the girls to clean up, created in us an appreciation deserving of more than a simple "Thank you." It was during such times that Anne Marie would often pick up a couple of thank you cards and write the girls a note on behalf of the two of us. Sometimes she would slip an inexpensive pair of earrings in with each card. This cost very little in time or money, yet it communicated our deep appreciation for their kindness and a desire on our part to celebrate our love for them. It also added quality the next time we said, "Thank you."

Whether you are working on reclaiming some lost ground or just working to improve your relationship, consider saying, "I appreciate you," with a simple gift. But there are some common pitfalls to avoid. Don't attach any "strings" or conditions to your gift. "I knew you would appreciate these new earrings, just like I'm going to appreciate seeing your room picked up more often." Such qualifiers rob the gift of its true meaning and suggest to the child that your motive for buying the gift was manipulative in the first place.

Genuine gifts from the heart are given without expectation in return. If you find yourself saying, "How could you do that after I gave you..." realize you're giving with expectations. And don't use it as a defense during later conflicts.

With Service

Closely associated with gift-giving is saying, "Thank you," through acts of service. In the incident above, we could also have expressed our thanks by doing something for the kids that we knew they would appreciate   something over and above what we would normally do.

The teen years were hectic in our home, and there were times when the girls' rooms showed it. Although the girls often kept them neat, there were seasons of clutter. Sometimes during these busy times, Anne Marie would clean their rooms. She wanted to say, "I love and appreciate you," in a tangible way. That act of service communicated the value we placed on what our children were giving to our lives. We appreciated it, and they knew it.

Quality Time

A fifth way to show encouragement to our teens is by giving them our time. As parents, we all struggle to balance competing demands. Work quotas, family responsibilities, personal interests, friendships, ministry opportunities, – all these and more cry out for our attention.

Your teen may very well be aware of the battle you wage. After all, he or she lives with you. Better than anyone else, your family knows how little time you have to spare. With that in mind, what could be more encouraging than to show up and cheer at your child's drama production, band concert, or soccer game? Or to take your teen to lunch one day, "Just to

tell you how proud I am of you, and the way you helped your brother study for his test" (made peace with your best friend, or prepared dinner on the night that Mom was sick)?

LET THEM WORK ON YOUR WEAKNESSES

Here is something to work on with your older middle years child. Invite your kids to work on your personal weaknesses. One characteristic of healthy families is the freedom granted each member to lovingly confront one another when necessary. The purpose of this confrontation is not to condemn but to strengthen. It is not to incite conflict but to provoke one another to love and good works (Hebrews 10:24).

The Holy Spirit provided the New Testament Church with a procedure permitting a believer to go to another in the Body of Christ to encourage and admonish him; this same strategy works for strengthening family relationships. "If a man is overtaken in any fault, you who are spiritual restore such a one in a spirit of gentleness, considering yourself lest you also be tempted" (Galatians 6:1). Notice the guidelines – you are to employ a spirit of gentleness, and are to remain aware of the power of sin over your own life.

We practiced this principle in our own family. Anne Marie and I knew we had parenting blind spots – wrong perspectives, lack of patience, occasional overconfidence in our decisions, or too little confidence in our children's. We knew our teens saw all our frailties. They knew our strengths and weaknesses. Realizing that no one desired that we know the truth more than our own children did, we invited, even encouraged them to help us become better human beings. In doing so, we communicated to our children that: 1) we trusted them, 2) we trusted their motives, and 3) we trusted their discernment. That trilogy spoke volumes to our daughters.

We didn't just let them have at it, though; we set up some guidelines governing this privilege. We'd like to share some guiding principles with you:

1. Teens cannot verbally assault their parents. They must speak honestly and honorably at the same time.
2. Both teens and parents must be in agreement on the particular weakness or weaknesses to be worked on.
3. Teens must come with a desire to help, not accuse; their motives must be morally focused.
4. Teens must be in control of their own attitudes when making an observation.
5. Struggling teens must want to start over. Their willingness to start over validates their desire to have a relationship with you.

There are some advantages to giving your teens the freedom to work on your weaknesses. First, it fosters within parents a healthy vulnerability. The popular notion is that vulnerability denotes weakness, but we're using the term to imply strength. One of the keys to unlocking the door to the human heart is healthy vulnerability. To be vulnerable is to be open to the healthy censure or criticism of mature members of the family. Morally mature members, that is. Vulnerability helps keep our inner person in check. It permits another person to hold up a mirror to our face so we can see who we really are and who we are becoming. When we hold the mirror to our own face, we tend to look only at our good side. Our teens are very good at showing us all sides. Teens detest hypocrisy in their parents; our vulnerability helps prevent it.

A second advantage comes by way of investment dividends paid out over time – relational dividends, that is. A number of years ago, a relative persuaded us to invest in a European company doing business in the United States. We bought their stock at $18 a share. Within a month our stock was worth $21 a share. Over the next several months, we watched our stock go up and down and back up again.

Getting involved in the stock market gave us a new appreciation for the word investment. Every day I found myself looking at the Dow Jones averages. My attention turned from what I did initially with my investment, to what I wanted to do with it, to what I felt I must do. I guarded and nurtured our shares. I remained focused on the returns. The more growth we saw in our investment, the more committed we became. If our returns began to diminish, our investment received renewed attention.

The same is true with relational investment. Giving our teens the freedom to work on our weaknesses allows them an opportunity to invest relationally and emotionally in us as well. There is one clear truth about human nature and the nature of investment: people tend not to walk away from an investment that cost a great deal. Personal investment gives us a reason to stick around – to nurture, watch, and add to our stock. Your teen will do that with you. But first you must give him a healthy prospect of real rewards for his investment – yourself.

Are you willing to be vulnerable and open to investment? How is your relational portfolio? Without those two attributes, your teen has no pathway to your heart and no hope for a healthy return.

These are just some of the many ways we can encourage our kids. But don't let the suggestions we've outlined limit you. Remember, any action that you do as a parent, which instills in your child the courage to do right, is encouragement. But there are wrong ways to encourage your middle years child. Here are some warnings.

THE DON'TS OF ENCOURAGEMENT

Parents must willfully work on proactive encouragement. How amazing it is to think that the ability to discourage good behavior is natural. Unfortunately, we tend to do it all the time. Here are some discouraging behaviors that you must try to avoid with your middle years children.

Don't Harp

Nothing can tune a kid out faster than when a parent constantly gripes about the child. For example, take the endless complaining about the half-frozen cat that was left out all night due to a teen's forgetfulness. The matter is brought up at breakfast, dinner, and again on the way home after youth group. It is revisited as the cat is tossed out the back door to take care of business before the family retires for the night. The lecture about the poor cat drones on and on. There is more to communicating with your children than lecturing on what they did wrong – again. Certainly, mistakes and sinful acts must be confronted, but if that is the only time you talk to your preteen, plan on being tuned out. Overtalk is communication overkill. We need to communicate effectively in order to teach the values governing personal responsibility. But harping is not an effective training method.

Don't Use Sarcasm

In an effort to draw attention to children's behavior, some parents use sarcasm in their daily conversation as a tool of coercion. Listen for the verbal barbs in these statements: "Well, with all the bread you are consuming, I guess you're not worried about your weight." "So, what kind of trouble did you get into at school today?" "When you act that way, I'm surprised you have any friends at all." I know parents who, in the past, constantly devalued their children by their lack of consideration and courtesy and their use of sarcasm. The end result is always the same: their kids grew bitter and resentful.

It's difficult to get preteens (or anyone, for that matter) to listen when they are treated disrespectfully. Older kids don't forget put-downs, and you can be sure the chickens will always come home to roost for the parent dishing them out. Turnoff words and put-down phrases force one of two reactions in teens. Either they verbally attack the source of irritation with their own sarcasm, or they withdraw in silence. In both cases the results are the same – our kids stop listening.

Some parents use sarcasm because they think it will help motivate their kids. But preteens and teens resist this type of "motivation" and become cynical of anything the parent says. This has a downward-spiraling effect in the future. Any new effort the parent puts forth to make amends is perceived as just another twisted effort to control the relationship, not build it.

Don't Rob Them of the Joy of Serving You

When talking about encouragement and gift-giving I shared earlier that Anne Marie and I have often rushed out to a meeting, leaving the kitchen in disarray. Coming home to a spotless kitchen without having prompted the girls to clean up was actually a normal occurrence. But sometimes we would say the wrong thing before leaving. "Girls could you clean up the table and do the dishes?" Those few words robbed our kids of the joy of serving us. By our request, we created personal expectations and removed the pleasant surprise that usually awaited us.

Our kids were characterized by cleaning up on our busy nights. They longed to hear our thankful appreciation when we walked back into the house to see the kitchen spotless. That was their joy. Those word: "Girls would you clean up the kitchen tonight?" instantly removed any possibility of serving us for no other reason than to love us. When your children are characterized by doing a special task, be careful not to rob them of the joy of doing it, by asking them in advance.

Beware of Hypocrisy

"You're nothing but a hypocrite!" This accusation is painful for any parent to bear. It's painful because there is usually some truth in the statement. If a parent lacks integrity, how can he or she be trusted? In fact, the cost of hypocrisy is trust. Parents who don't live by the moral values they set up for the rest of the family fall into this category – they're untrustworthy. In the sentence above, the key word is moral. During the early years of childhood, parental authority, although challenged, is not questioned in terms of parental integrity.

For example, parents tell their children not to cross the street, light a fire, let the dog run loose, or climb the ladder. Yet parents do all these things without their actions being perceived as hypocritical, because these activities in and of themselves are not intrinsically moral in nature. But when it comes to moral instruction and moral behavior, no disparity should exist between what parents teach and what they do. The moral rules the child is taught to live by are the same for the parent. Adulthood does not come with a new set of values; moral truth does not vary with our age. You can be sure teens make moral judgments on the behavior of friends, school mates, and teachers, using the standards taught them by their parents. It should not surprise us, then, when our teens use those same standards to judge us.

SUMMARY

This chapter has focused on how you can be a good encourager to your kids and how to avoid discouraging them. In our next chapter, we will take up a potpourri of discipline topics pertaining to the middle years child.

Questions for Review

1. Explain the main difference between encouraging younger children versus middle years children.

2. Give a couple of examples (other than what was given in the reading) of what it means to qualify your encouragement.

3. Explain the two advantages gained when you let your kids work on your personal weaknesses.

4. How do parents rob their children of the joy of serving them?

5. What is the cost of hypocrisy?

9

Discipline Potpourri

Whenever we talk to parents of preschoolers, sooner or later all questions seem to lead to, "How should I discipline them?" Young parents want to know the best methods of controlling their children, how to establish and reinforce rules, and how to punish. We find it interesting that when talking to parents of preteens and teens, sooner or later all of their questions eventually lead to, "How should I discipline them?"

There seems to be a prevailing assumption that if parents can master better methods of punishment, whether it be for a preschooler or an adolescent, they will solve their parent-teen conflicts. Surely punishment plays a role in child training, but in the teen years it plays a greatly diminished role.

We can't count how many times we have listened to parents struggling with disciplining their older children. Sometimes parents get the mistaken idea that if they figure out exactly how to punish more effectively, that will "fix" every problem. As we go through this chapter, remember that correction is only one part of the training process. Both correction and encouragement are most effective in the context of healthy relationships. Don't expect correction to fix all problems, but view it as one of the tools to help shape your child's heart.

BACK TO BASICS

The reason we bring correction into the lives of our preteens and teens is basic. Correction helps them learn. But in order for the correction to be tied to learning, we need to understand the two rules of correction.

This is the first rule: *The type of correction depends on the presence or absence of evil motive.* Parents should ask, "Was my preteen's wrong action accidental or intentional? The answer to that question determines which type of correction is appropriate. This is the dividing line. Bad decisions and accidents bring natural consequences, but intentional moral violations affecting other people require punishment. There is a difference between bringing consequences into the life of your teen and punishing your teen.

As parents, we need to understand punishment from a biblical perspective, not a societal one. Society punishes to get even and exact revenge; God does not. He is not vindictive, nor does He seek to even the score. His purpose for punitive correction is precise – to bring about the peaceable fruit of righteousness (Hebrews 12:11).

In adulthood, we do not get punished for

our decisions; instead, we learn life's lessons by living with the correctness or incorrectness of our choices. So should it be with our older preteens. Because this child is closer to adulthood than childhood, the need for punishment should sharply drop, while the use of natural and logical consequences will become the more common method employed during correction.

There is a difference between punishment and natural and logical consequences. Because moral truth is imparted during early childhood, punishment will be used more than natural or logical consequences. Punishment serves a moral purpose. It communicates to children the value of good and evil by the weight of punishment ascribed to each wrongful act. In contrast, the use of natural and logical consequences in child training does not communicate values but has as a goal the training in personal responsibility.

The second rule of correction is this: *The punishment/consequences must fit the crime.* Punishment sets a value on behavior. That is why over-punishing or under-punishing is dangerous. Both send the wrong message.

When we as a society – or as parents – establish a punishment, we are making a value statement. We are determining the degree and seriousness of a wrongful act. Punishment places a value on evil offenses. It is important to note that a child's sense of justice is established through punishment, not rewards. For example, if a child hits and bruises his sister with a plastic bat and then is punished with five minutes in the time-out chair, the parent has just established in the mind of the child that hurting other people is not that serious an infraction.

Unjust punishments can go to the other extreme, too. When a parent says, "You left your

light on after leaving your room and for that, you can't play your radio for a month," he is over-punishing his child. This fosters exasperation and more conflict.

Before an offense can be dealt with most effectively, the parent needs to ask two questions: "Was what my child did the result of an accident, or was it malicious? What punishment would fit the wrong done and convey the right value message?"

At this point we would encourage you to review the discipline chapters of *Growing Kids God's Way.* Many of the basic principles found there will apply to the middle years. Meanwhile, we will move forward with a potpourri of new age-appropriate discipline concepts. Here are five important considerations for your middle years child.

CORRECTING PERSONAL ATTITUDES

Not long ago, a young father asked me how he could best punish his son for displaying jealousy. That specific question leads to a broader one. How do you correct the sinful attitudes of the heart? What do you do with envy, revenge, spitefulness, and jealousy? How do you help your child overcome the fleshly impulses of their humanity?

Because of their age, middle years children are better served by *substitution* than *suppression.* The father mentioned above was frustrated by his efforts to suppress his son's jealousy. No matter how hard he tried to keep the lid on it, jealousy continued to leak out. Instead of suppressing the wrong, we encourage you to substitute the opposite virtue. When dealing with your child's abstract feelings as opposed to concrete behavior, correction comes not solely by suppressing the wrong attitude but by elevating and teaching the opposite virtue. Suppression of wrong is often achieved by substituting the right. In the case of suppressing jealousy, give equal time to elevating the opposite virtue – contentment.

If you have a child struggling with envy, teach charity; for anger, teach self-control; for revenge, teach forgiveness. Substitution, not just suppression, will make all the difference in the world. Our young father above did just that. His son's jealousy was mastered by his son's new-found freedom in contentment.

TEACH TOMORROW'S CONSEQUENCES

Teach your children concretely by showing them tomorrow's consequences for today's decisions. The operative word above is *concretely*. There are some examples that must be absorbed by the senses if our children are to learn their lesson.

Matty and Toby, although fun to play with, were not trained to be responsible children. Our kids knew that from previous experiences. One Saturday afternoon while visiting Amy and Jenny, the four decided to play house. But instead of playing upstairs in the girls' rooms, Matty and Toby convinced Amy and Jenny to set up house outside in the woods.

Anne Marie and I gave one warning: "Girls, everything you take out must be returned." "Okay, Mom and Dad," came the response. We knew how this was going to turn out, and our kids should have known how this was going to turn out as well.

Amy, Jenny, Matty, and Toby began hauling small tables and chairs, stoves, and sinks to the woods alongside the house. It didn't take long before an Alice in Wonderland tea party began. The kids had neatly placed little plates on the table, with knives, forks, and napkins. The kitchen had pans on the stove, dishes alongside the sink, and rocking chairs filled with stuffed animals – all under a natural canopy of oak and maple trees.

The kids weren't out there more than ten minutes when Toby and Matty's Mom called them home. It was happening. In that moment, the girls realized the mistake they had made.

Their request for help with returning everything to the house was greeted with an out-of-character desire from Toby and Matty to give their mother immediate obedience. "We gotta go, our mother is calling." The two left Amy and Jenny sitting there with every item to put back themselves.

Anne Marie and I could have helped. We could have come alongside the girls, picked up some of their toys, and tried to teach into the moment. But we purposely chose not to. We wanted this lesson to saturate their senses. We directed the girls to return everything back to their rooms, just as they found them. When they were done, we sat and talked about unreliable friends. Our kids knew that Matty and Toby were unreliable, yet they did not act on their discernment.

Every trip back to their rooms sealed a lesson that would serve them for life. The wise do not take counsel from fools, nor should you believe their promises. One only needs to look at the fields of the fool to see where their counsel will lead (Proverbs 24:30-32). Teach your middle years children by showing them concretely tomorrow's consequences for today's decisions.

MICRO AND MACRO REBELLION

In *GKGW*, we defined rebellion as acts and attitudes of willful defiance. Included in this definition are disobeying, talking back, refusing to accept correction, or rejecting rightful authority. Most kids demonstrate open rebellion. That is, when they cross the line, they cross it all the way. We call this *macro rebellion* – macro meaning large in contrast to small. For example, you tell your son to put the ball down gently, but instead he throws it at his sister. Or, you call your child to you and he ignores you by running off in the opposite direction. These examples demonstrate what we mean by macro rebellion. There are a certain number of children who do not rebel in such obvious ways but rather are content to just put their toe over the line. These children fall into the *micro rebellious* category. That is, their wrongful deeds are not clamorous, revealing, or as openly defiant as the macro child but rather just an inch over the line. The micro child is one who, instead of running away when called, will come over to you but only half-way. This is the child, who when asked to put the ball down, will put it in his pocket. When asked to stay out of the kitchen, he will place his feet on the carpet with his toes just across the floor tiles.

One distinguishing characteristic of this child is the fact that he or she rarely crosses the line in a macro sense. And that becomes part of the problem. Because the sin of the micro child just doesn't look too bad when contrasted with the sin of macro rebellious siblings, parents tend to underestimate the seriousness of the offense, dismissing it as just another minor infraction. But it is not a minor infraction to the child. For the micro child, the toe over the line is one hundred percent, pure rebellion.

A second problem follows on the heels of the first. The Bible says, "Because the sentence against an evil work is not executed speedily, therefore the heart of the sons of men is fully set in them to do evil" (Ecclesiastes 8:11). The results are found in verses 12 and 13, "Though a sinner does evil a hundred times and his days are prolonged, yet I surely know that it will be well with those who fear God who fear before Him. But it will not be well with the wicked, nor will he prolong his days which are as a shadow, because he does not fear before God." The micro child has a false sense of God's judgment. Because the offense is dismissed as slight, the lack of correction breeds contempt for your authority.

If you have a micro rebellious child who is still in the middle years, work diligently with his sin, lest his sin give him a false sense of comfort and confidence. We are fearful that the dreaded consequences will show up during the teen years.

PARENTING FROM THE YOUNGEST UP

Remember Paul's admonishment in Ephesians 6:4a? "And Fathers, do not exasperate your children. . ." Here is one way parents do this: by shackling middle years children with the restraints placed on younger children. This is parenting to the lowest common denominator, or from the youngest up. The fear that the younger child will not understand or will seek the freedoms of the older child causes some parents to pull back on age-appropriate freedoms, creating a condition of frustration.

As one mom told us: "Everything is going so well. I'm afraid if I let up on the oldest, the younger children will not understand why they don't have the same privileges." This mom needs to tell the younger children that when they become as responsible as their older brother or sister, they too will have those special privileges.

We usually spot this problem in the manner by which parents lead their children. As discussed in Chapter Two, by the time your kids approach adolescence, you should be well on your way to leading by your influence and less by the power of your authority. Too often the exact opposite takes place. Coercive parental authority is still the primary way of controlling the child. It shouldn't be, and it will backfire on you. Do not parent your oldest child out of the fear of what the youngest might think.

HELPFUL HINTS FOR DOING CHORES
Recently a friend of the ministry, Connie Hadidian, shared with us this creative approach to accomplishing family chores for her middle years children. For the children's chores she used a 3 x 5 index card system. The children are handed their chore cards each morning, given a time limit, and given the responsibility of finishing their chores within the time limit. All need for nagging or prodding, and hurry-up warning is removed, thus providing a very pleasant atmosphere, especially during the usual morning family rush hour.

What do you need to get started?

- Colored 3 x 5 index cards – one color for each child of chore age and two extra color cards
- Index card box
- 3 x 5 dividers
- Black writing marker

Connie divided her chore card box into four sections. She uses pink cards for Marissa's personal tasks, such as making her bed, brushing her teeth, picking up her room, etc. Blue cards are for Matthew's personal tasks. Green cards represent chores that both children are capable of doing, - sweeping the kitchen floor, emptying all trash, wiping down sliding door, folding laundry, taking out trash, and so on. And peach colored cards (the two extra color cards), say, "See Mom for a treat."

Using Matthew as an example, here is how it works. Each morning Matthew's chore cards are placed out for him, (on the kitchen table or counter). This consist of his blue cards and some green cards. The stove timer goes on for an appropriate amount of time. Matthew works through his cards, flipping each face down when the task is completed until all chores are done. They must be done before the timer goes off.

Each card section contains chores that not only need to be done daily, but weekly and monthly, such as taking sheets off the bed, cleaning out desk drawers, and sweeping the patio. Some of the weekly or monthly chores are given after school and not during the regular chore time.

In the stack of chore cards for each child, there is one that reads, "See Mom if you think you are done." This card is helpful for two reasons. First, it lets you know if the chores are done before the stove timer goes off, and second, you can check to see if the job is done to your satisfaction.

Every once in a while, a peach colored card is thrown in – "See Mom for a treat." When the children discover this with great delight, then express your feelings of appreciation for how well they are doing. The special treat might be going out for ice cream, going out to a restaurant, or receiving a dollar bill.

If you have young children who do not read yet, put a picture, stamp, or sticker on each card to represent the chore next to simple words describing the chore. For example, put a picture of a bed next to the words, "make bed." For the little ones, it takes about a week before they are doing their little chores independently and successfully. Here are some advantages to this method.

- It takes only a few minutes each morning to gather the children's chore cards for the day.
- It teaches the children responsibility and self-discipline.
- Younger children can participate.
- The system is flexible. You can add or delete chores as needed and as the child grows older.

A final word about motivation. We again remind you that simply getting outward performance is not the goal of your parenting, but the goal is to help create a servant's heart in your children. Chores are one way to teach the virtue of *otherness*. Your children need to feel they are welcome and contributing members of your family. Having them do chores is one way to accomplish this.

Questions for Review

1. What are the two rules of correction?

2. How is punishment related to values?

3. Explain how you would correct personal attitudes with substitution rather than suppression.

4. Do you have a micro rebellious child? If you think you do, explain why.

5. Explain the following statement: "Do not parent to the lowest common denominator".

10

Looking Ahead to Dating and Courtship

We actually stand amazed at how often we thought about dropping this chapter, but retreated from all the voices of protest. Apparently parents of middle schoolers desire this information sooner than later. Although your middle years child will not be courting or dating for a number of years, it appears that it is not too soon to start thinking about the process. How should you be directing your child's thinking on this subject? The first rule is this. Don't say to your middle years child, "When you're sixteen you can date." Sixteen is going to come quickly enough, and by the time your child gets there you will probably be sorry you set any age for dating. To understand the dynamics of courtship and dating, it will be helpful to return to the Bible and first century

Actually, the Bible doesn't offer specific guidelines for courtship or dating, although courtship (and probably dating to some extent) was practiced by the Jews in the first century. The only premarriage custom spoken of in the Bible was betrothment, meaning to pledge to marry or to become engaged.

The word "betroth" speaks of a marriage commitment of a son or daughter. It appears throughout the Law of Moses (Exodus 21:8-9; Leviticus 19:20; Deuteronomy 22:25, 28:30)

and is also used poetically by the prophets. In the Old Testament book of Hosea the Lord said "I will betroth you to Me forever; Yes, I will betroth you to Me in righteousness and justice, in loving kindness and mercy. I will betroth you to Me in faithfulness, and you shall know the Lord" (Hosea 2:19-20).

If you look for a definitive statement in the Bible on the methods and timing of betrothment or courtship, there are none. What we know of these practices comes from the study of early Jewish customs. But Jewish customs should not be viewed as a substitute for biblical revelation because neither tradition or practice can equate to God breathed revelation.

Jewish historians considered betrothment to be a formal act of property transfer, wherein the groom gave his bride's family money or something else of monetary value to secure her. In return, someone from the bride's family (usually the father) gave a written declaration, which became known as the *marriage contract*. Although it has no biblical commendation, the "marriage contract" containing the "marriage agreement" has survived two millenniums.

In 1828, Noah Webster's *American Dictionary of the English Language* defined *betroth* as "a contract for future marriage, done either by a father for his daughter or by a man contracting a future wife."

Anne Marie's grandmother's betrothal contract of April 13, 1906, notarized in Boston, Massachusetts, hangs on the wall in our upstairs bedroom. In it, Anne Marie Salza of Avellino Province, Italy agreed to marry Pietro Perrino of Boston, Massachusetts when she came to America. Both parties signed the contract. The contract clause of betrothal survived into the 1940s where it appeared in 1942 in the *Webster Consolidated Dictionary*. Over the next twenty years, however, the popular meaning of betrothment, with the marriage contract clause, began to change. By the mid-1960s the contract element was dropped in many dictionaries, returning the word to its original Hebrew meaning: an agreement to marry – to be engaged.

DATING AND COURTSHIP

In 1828, Noah Webster defined *dating* as, "knowing the time of happening or to assign a date to an event or letter." Now, approximately a hundred seventy-five years later, modern dictionaries define dating as "a social engagement with persons of the opposite sex." The fact that teens didn't date a hundred seventy-five years ago does not make dating wrong – just different from times past. Dating must be judged on its merits, not on its existence. Is there any specific merit or potential harm with dating as practiced in our culture?

Before we can answer that question, we must contrast the act of dating with courtship. "Courtship" or "courting" was defined by Noah Webster as "the act of wooing; solicitation of a woman to marriage." That meaning has changed very little since Webster's time. Today, the *American Heritage Dictionary* defines courtship as "an act of seeking to gain love or affection

with a view toward marriage."

Courting and dating are not synonymous. Here are some important differences to note:

1. Courtship assumes and requires age-readiness for marriage. The nature of cultural dating does not.

2. Courtship presupposes the possibility of an actual mature love relationship that will lead to engagement. Cultural dating makes no such assumption.

3. Courtship is a personal and mutual commitment of two people willing to investigate the possibility of marriage. Cultural dating often occurs largely because the peer group expects it, rather than as the outcome of a real personal interest on the part of the adolescent. It also sometimes is used to fulfill selfish desires.

4. Courtship considers factors beyond just the couple such as parents, family and extended family, belief systems, values, and personal convictions. Cultural dating has a single focus – the activity of dating itself.

5. Courtship is a means to an end, which is called engagement. Cultural dating is an end unto itself.

Courtship then is the prelude to a possible engagement. Its purpose is to provide a couple time to discover, assess, and evaluate their compatibility as potential lifelong marriage partners. Courtship isn't a time of experimentation but of exploration. Cultural dating, on the other hand, is a modern social experience allowing teens to have premature access to a serious male/female relationship, something previously reserved only for courting.

Because the activity of courtship is not a guarantee of engagement or marriage but a controlled step toward it, it must have some objective guides that will allow either party to stop the process or at least slow it down. Courtship is not a linear concept. It doesn't necessarily start at point A and conveniently end at point Z with no rivers or valleys in between. Along the way there are variables that can emotionally and spiritually stretch both participants in ways they have never before experienced. The closer two people grow together, the more the underlying, and not necessarily pleasant, habits begin to show themselves. That's why neither child nor parent should rush into courtship without the ability and recourse to stop the process. Both need to be able to rein in the relationship, if necessary.

DATING VERSUS ESCORTING

When it comes to dating versus courtship, it isn't a case that one is right and the other is wrong. Dating is not inherently right or wrong. Anne Marie and I still date each other. Our married children enjoy their "date night." What makes dating acceptable or unacceptable is the age of participants, the appropriateness of the relationship, the context of dating, and the motive for dating.

While we would not encourage any form of romantic dating outside of courtship, we do recognize dating as a critical element of courtship. Courtship is what qualifies and legitimizes the dating experience. Courtship validates dating by providing the necessary context. Dating is part of the courting process. The dating experience should not be independent of courtship, but rather dependent upon and submissive to its purpose.

If dating is part of courtship, is there ever a time when a son or daughter can be with the opposite sex in a date-like setting outside of courtship? We believe the answer is yes. Our children chose not to date during their high school years. They accepted their mother's counsel, realizing that dating does not serve a spiritual purpose and too often leads to trouble. However, there *were* circumstances that allowed them to go out with a boy in a date-like setting.

My daughter Amy's ninth-grade banquet was a special event. She dined in the beautifully decorated school gymnasium with the rest of her class. The young man who accompanied her was not her date. He was her *escort* for the evening. A similar event took place when she was a senior in high school. She was escorted to the school banquet by a young man whom we met and approved of. It was a fun event but a one-time occurrence. There was no commitment on either side beyond the evening. The difference between an escorted event and a date is found in the purpose.

There will always be some unique situations in which a boy might escort a girl to an event without it having to be a boyfriend-girlfriend date. There are five common characteristics of an escort companion that stand in contrast to a date:

1. Escorting is rare and is usually tied to a function, while dating is often frequently occurring and not tied to any special event.

2. Escorting places no emotional commitment on the other party. Dating does.

3. Escorting is not part of a boyfriend-girlfriend relationship. Dating usually is.

4. The escort for different events does not need to be the same person. Dating couples often do not change partners (not until one partner feels it is time to break up the relationship and perhaps take a new partner in a dating relationship).

5. Escorting does not create the possibility of emotional fraud. Dating allows a teen to entertain the idea of love and romance with one who probably will never be that teen's lifelong mate.

In conclusion, we don't believe it is wise that teens become involved in the dating experience outside of courtship. Allowing young people to date under circumstances that can lead to temptation – which may result in intimacies, early love relationships, and sexual excitement and experimentation – often leads to serious difficulties in the future. Such dating can defraud the future mate.

In 1 Corinthians 7:1-5, the apostle Paul spoke on sexual purity. In this text he highlighted one significant truth – marital dominion. The wife does not have full authority over her own body nor does the husband over his. (1 Corinthians 7:4). Paul admonished each one to possess his or her own body in view of the dominion rights of the other. Marital dominion means there is a title deed of ownership on our bodies held in part by our mates. We are to do nothing that violates that ownership.

Ownership in this case is not bound by time. Our children managed their bodies in sanctification and honor long before they met their future husbands. They did so believing that time was the only barrier to their relationship. The fact that they, in their singleness, did not know who their mates would be

only increased their passion for purity. Your children must be made aware that they can defraud their future husband or wife while in their state of singleness. For too many teens, dating is like sampling a box of chocolates – they take a bite out of each one, making them all undesirable.

THE THREE PHASES OF COURTSHIP

When a child reaches a marriageable age and courtship begins, keep in mind that it is a family matter, not just a young couple's event. It is an unfolding process, a revelation of souls – not only the souls of the children, but those of both sets of parents. We discovered with our children that courtship naturally unfolds in three phases – exploration, confirmation, and pledging. Each phase brings a new level of responsibility and unique challenges to the couple, and each phase allows for either person to pull in the reins and slow down the process.

Phase One: Exploration

Courtship is not for strangers. Only after your son or daughter develops a friendship should courtship be considered. To enter the exploration phase of courtship is to acknowledge that marriage is a possibility but not a promise. The basic purpose of this phase is to allow the couple to explore and discover their own emotions beyond that of simple friendship. Through their courting experience, the young couple learns to rearrange their lives for the benefit of each other, developing the pleasant while modifying the unpleasant aspects of their personalities. Common likes and dislikes are discovered, reinforced, and clarified. They leave this phase seeking concrete meaning and understanding for their new feelings.

Phase Two: Confirmation

This phase brings both young people face to face with the need to reveal themselves and to be revealed. Yet at the same time, another more powerful force brings pressure to bear, to hide and foil the process of personal discovery – personal pride. Pride always attempts to foil discovery or at least taint the truth about ourselves. During the process of confirmation, the couple learns lessons of give and take, overcoming frustrations, and handling jealousies, insecurities, misunderstandings, and the exaltation of the other. All this aids the process of confirming their selection. Through it all, sufficient confidence is achieved in the expression of each other's love to declare the relationship publicly. It is in the latter stages of this second phase that the foundation of marriage is actually realized. The couple's new love provides a pleasant response that symbolizes a unity of feeling. It is accompanied by the exclusive experiences of shared confidences, secrets, future plans, and all the other elements that make up the uniqueness of two people in love.

Phase Three: Pledging

This is the time of pledging, when a new community is created deep in the soul. During this phase of emotional maturation, the image of marriage is exchanged for the reality. There is absolute solidarity of thinking and feelings toward each other. Not only is there solidarity, but there is a natural interdependence between the two, wherein they continually complement one another through their efforts. They achieved a marriage of their souls that only awaits the calendar date.

TEN GUIDELINES FOR COURTING

We found these guidelines to be helpful for us and our children. They are suggestions that allowed our daughters to have access to us, and us to them, when it came to their periods of courting.

1. Courting does not take place until after friendship compatibility is established.

2. Courting takes place after both families meet each young adult.

3. Prior to the first time the two are out alone together, the young man must ask the girl's father for permission to take her out.

4. The parents should know the couple's itinerary for the evening.

5. The courting couple must individually be working on their relationship with God more than their relationship with the other person.

6. A couple can never be in either's home alone.

7. The young man must continually inform the girl's parents of each new level of emotional growth experienced by the couple in the courtship.

8. There should be no extended time alone in a parked car.

9. Purity in the relationship must be protected at all times.

10. Respect should be shown to the calendar of activities of both families with regard to nights out. Courting cannot take away

from other activities – family night, school, ministry, and church.

SAVING YOUR HEART

Preparation for marriage starts long before a child reaches maturity. His or her heart still needs protection, guidance, and oversight. In marriage we use a ring as a symbol of our personal commitment to one another. It becomes a continual reminder of our love and devotion. But such commitment and devotion should not be developed only after a mate is secured. Years before your children say, "I do," at their weddings, they should pledge their purity to the one yet to come with whom they will share life. They are pledging to remain pure and undefiled until God brings that special person into their life.

How can you help hold your children accountable to the task? What can you do in a non-coercive way to encourage their purity and remind them of their pledge? Here is a beautiful example of how one father helped his daughter guard her heart for marriage and her future mate. While the age in this story is thirteen, other parents waited until their daughter was fifteen or sixteen.

On the occasion of her thirteenth birthday, a father planned a special date with his daughter. Their time together would be so special that it would be difficult, if not impossible, for his daughter to ever forget it. The father's purpose for the grand evening was to encourage her to commit herself to a life of purity during the all-important teen years. After plans were made, the special day finally arrived. Early that morning, her mother presented her with a gold key, along with instructions to give the key as a gift to her father after he had given his gift to

her. The mother assured her daughter that she would then understand why she was to give away her birthday present.

That evening, the father arrived to pick up his daughter in a borrowed, chauffeur-driven Mercedes. His daughter was nervous but excited about her "first date" – with Dad. He had planned and saved for months for this special date. The ride to the restaurant was filled with light, enjoyable conversation as Dad and daughter recounted many of the fun events of the past.

After dinner, the father asked his daughter if he could share his heart with her. He began by reminding her that the Lord called her to a life of purity and holiness—"Be ye Holy for I am Holy" (1 Peter 1:16) – which would be the very best for her life. And as her father, he too wanted God's best for her life, he told her. He then went on to explain that she would be facing many new challenges in the years to come, one of which would be developing relationships with boys. The father further explained that the Lord had given him the joy and responsibility of watching over and protecting his daughter, especially during the teen years. After she understood what was involved, her father asked that she make a commitment to the Lord that she would allow her dad to watch over her and protect her during her teen years.

At that moment the father pulled out his gift and gave it to her. As she opened the gift, she found a beautiful gold heart on a gold chain. As the father placed the chain about her neck, he explained to her that the gold heart represents her purity in life. At that moment, she gave her dad the gift of the key, and understood that in giving the key to her dad she was saying, "Yes Dad, I want you to have the key to my heart, to protect it and keep it safe."

The father experienced inexpressible joy as he said to her, "I will guard the key to your heart and all that it represents until the day of your wedding – then I will give it to your husband."

A similar event can take place with a son, with only minor changes. The message is the same–calling the child to a personal commitment to holiness and purity. You are attempting to build a memory for the night that will last through the teen years, so select a place that is very special. The dinner this time will be with Dad, Mom, and son. Instead of a locket and a key, the father after dinner gives his son a beautiful women's necklace. The necklace is then given by the son to the woman God has given him to love and honor - his mother. The mother is to wear the necklace as a continual reminder of his pledge of purity and commitment to the girl who will someday be his wife. In exchange, the mother gives the son a gold ring engraved with the date of his pledge. The ring serves as a continual reminder of his pledge to personal purity and holiness. On the son's wedding day, the mother gives the necklace to his bride, symbolizing the fulfillment of their commitment and his pledge. The son gives the ring to his father-in-law and mother-in-law, signifying his personal commitment to their daughter.

Whether it be for a daughter or son, the locket, ring, and necklace are only reminders of a pledge. So we want to remind you that it is not the ceremony or the objects that assure commitment to these vows, but the steady loving encouragement from Mom and Dad. It all gets back to having healthy relationships with your children. The rewards of doing so are beyond description.

Questions For Review

1. What specific guidelines does the Bible offer regarding courtship and dating?

2. What is dating and how do you feel about it for your child?

3. What is the primary difference between dating and courtship, and how do you feel about it?

4. What are the three phases of courtship?

11

Seven Warning Flags

For one who so greatly enjoys ice fishing, living in southern California has one obvious drawback – there's no ice. I remember my ice fishing days on our lake in New Hampshire. The sport could be the biggest bore when nothing was happening or the greatest thrill when the fish were striking. The signal that a fish struck my bait was the release of a red flag that would spring back and forth against the backdrop of white snow. The swaying flag called for immediate attention. Something was happening below the surface.

In middle years parenting, there are certain red flags to look out for. They are signaling that something is happening below the visible water line of your child's life. To ignore these warnings can lead to troublesome years ahead. Here are seven warning flags to consider.

WARNING FLAG ONE:
Your child does not follow the family standard outside of your presence (or the presence of others who know and represent your family values).

We realize there is no such thing as absolute moral consistency among adults, let alone children. There is always a degree of discrepancy between one's personal moral code and his or her behavior. But when your middle years child becomes characterized by not caring who sees him or what he is doing, especially when he is around people who are familiar with your family's values, then the child's problem is one of shame – the lack of it.

Shame, like empathy, is a moral emotion and one often confused with embarrassment. It shouldn't be. Shame and embarrassment, although similar are not the same thing. A woman during an interview notices a run in her nylons and immediately feels embarrassed. But there is no moral right or wrongness to her situation.

In contrast, shame is triggered by moral circumstances. Before the Fall of Man, Adam and Eve were in the garden and, "They were not ashamed," (Genesis 2:25). Shame is a mechanism of the conscience and acts as a restrainer of wrong behavior when personal moral conviction fails. That is, when the virtues of the soul are not sufficient to restrain temptation, God, out of protection for the society, provides the socializing tool of shame.

Many people are restrained from doing evil because they do not want social judgment to fall on them. Thus, shame becomes a societal safety net when personal moral resolve is gone.

Shame is motivated by the fear of judgment on one's conduct more than the individual's love of virtue.

Here is an example of what I mean. A friend of mine has his company name, "Bob's Lighting" abbreviated on his license plate. It reads BOBLITES. He is fairly well known around town, so people often recognize his pickup truck. In a casual conversation, I asked him if it held him more accountable to the speed limit His response was shamefully honest. "Yes, it does," he said. "I tend to drive faster than the law permits at times. But now that I have my license vanity plate on, I begin to think, what if people see me? I would be ashamed if they thought of me as a traffic violator."

In Bob's case, his desire to do wrong was negated, not out of his love for virtue, but the fear of shame associated with being caught by the public. My friend is not alone. We all operate from a degree of potential shame. Shamefully, there are certain moral temptations that we turn away from because the impulse of public judgment is greater than the hatred within our souls for the sin.

The moral makeup of our society complicates the problem even more. Today, our society is ruled by moral relativism. That means shame is no longer wanted or desired. If there are no absolute standards governing moral decency, into what context does shame respond? Without moral absolutes, no behavior can be shameful.

And that brings us back to your middle years child. When a child does not follow the family standard outside of your presence or the presence of others who know and represent your family values, it is an indication that he has no shame. Certainly, we were children, we did things outside the view of our parents, but shame restrained us from doing wrong in front of adults who knew us and our parents. We were conscious of bringing shame to our parents and family. Today, the voice of shame, the safety net of our conscience, is lost. Make sure it's found in your child.

WARNING FLAG TWO:
Your child tends to enjoy friends more than his or her own family. He or she is always asking to bring a friend on family activities.

Children are social beings. They love companionship. At first, children merely want to do things with others. Those who satisfy this desire are playmates. As a child grows older, he seeks more than playmates – he seeks friends. As he matures into pre- and early adolescence, outside interests begin to expand and attachment to friends becomes deeper. But should outside friendships replace those inside the family? The answer of course is no. But it does happen.

If a child's family offers him little satisfaction, he is deprived of the most important sources of emotional security his sense of belonging. When middle years children fail to find relational satisfaction at home, they turn outward to peers.

Parents need to be careful not to confuse a child's outward compliance to family rules as a mark of a healthy relationship. While it might be true that your child is really a good kid, responds well, and knows all the right *GKGW* things to do, you must understand that such good behavior is not necessarily a true measurement of a good relationship. One clue to this condition is seen in whether or not your child is constantly in need of peer companionship, even during family times. The warning flag is pointing to your family structure. Are you cultivating an *interdependent* family, or have you drifted toward the *independent* family?

Children who are accustomed to receiving comfort and approval from a few intimate and dependable relationships, such as found in the interdependent family, tend to look to those same or similar relationships for comfort and companionship as they move through adolescence. If this is not the case with your child, take inventory of your family structure.

WARNING FLAG THREE:
The peer group that your child is attracted to comes from families that do not share your values.

Over sixteen years ago, we crossed the United States by car heading for Los Angeles, camping along the way. We pulled in to our last camp site at 6:30 p.m. on July 18, 1983. Sitting up on a rise ten miles outside of the city of Las Vegas, our last KOA facility overlooked the brown heat waves rising from the city.

It was nearly nightfall when I finished pitching the tent. The business of the evening kept us occupied – so much so that we failed to notice the transformation of the city below. It was only after we sat down at our picnic table that we saw to the west the mysterious, luring lights of Las Vegas. We sat amazed – more than amazed. We sat charmed, enchanted by the glittering scene below. Las Vegas was calling us to investigate her glamour.

Four thousand years ago another man pitched his tent on an elevated plain toward a city. His name was Lot. The city was Sodom. Surely that city did not have the values that Lot's uncle Abraham had, but nonetheless, Lot still found the city attractive, so much so that he left the plains and moved to the city to take up a new identity.

What drives a child to homes of differing values? Two things: First, the inherent attraction to that which is different, and second, the natural bent of some children to the more colorful aspects of life. This warning concerns itself with a possible misplaced identity, which leads futuristically to a misplaced allegiance.

Identity is a socializing process by which a person identifies himself with a group he is familiar with, attracted to, or feels empathy for. Identity defines us by providing a set of socially understood reference points. A parish priest, for example, has a religious identity revealed in his clothing, speech, and lifestyle. The rock musician also is recognized by his clothing, speech, and lifestyle. They both have an identity that complements their values, and they both are identified by what they believe and how they act. People don't look at the rock musician and say, "Ah, there goes a religious man," nor do they look at the priest and say, "There goes a pop singer."

Our identity associations reveal us for who we are and what we believe. And that is why parents need to monitor the types of peer attraction their child is drawn to. This may be a red flag warning that your family identity is not all that it should be.

WARNING FLAG FOUR:
You're hearing similar negative reports from a number of different people about your child.

"No, my son doesn't really lie," said the mother. "He's just a creative story-teller." Our school administrator was not the first one to approach this parent about Brian's dishonesty. Over time, many others had echoed a similar concern. Ever since his preschool days, Brian's appetite for the convenience of dishonesty was continually dismissed by Mom and Dad. Only when the police started routinely knocking on the door did Brian's parents start to listen. By then it was too late. Their refusal to investigate, let alone accept, any criticism of their son's behavior helped shape him into a pathological liar.

It is humbling, embarrassing, and sometimes shameful to hear negative reports about our children. Every inch of pride wants to dismiss the possibility that what we are hearing is true. To receive criticism about ourselves is never pleasant. To receive criticism about our children is painful. But if you are living and participating in a moral community, such rebuke is an expression of God's grace. He cares for us. God sends people to us to warn and rebuke us. The Bible says, "Faithful are the wounds of a friend" (Proverbs 27:6).

Do not be like Israel. For when the prophets came to speak to their sin, they were dismissed and their words had no meaning, until the day of calamity. When friends start to bring similar reports to you about your child, listen to them.

WARNING FLAG FIVE:
Although it might be done in a playful way, your child is continually seeking attention from the opposite sex.

This is a warning flag to Dad. There is simply not enough physical touch taking place. Holding our children provides more than security – it meets special emotional needs that someday will be met when the Lord Himself brings that special person into their lives. Fathers who fail to communicate love through touch leave behind yearning hearts that can be taken captive by anyone willing to give atten-

tion. And often it's the wrong person.

In the course of our travels, we visit many families. In some homes we find children starved for physical affection. It's not that the parents are purposely neglectful, but that the tyranny of the urgent dominates their lives, and their children's need for touch goes unmet. Sometimes we are not in a home more than five minutes before we have children on our laps seeking to be cuddled. Silently they are asking us, "Would you hold me? My Dad is too busy." Many little boys and girls who have all the material things of life lack what they really need – a routine embrace from Dad.

As your children approach the teen years, they will have an interest in the opposite sex – that is the natural way. As a result, some flirtation is normal and a certain amount should be expected. But is your child seeking sexual attention? This red flag calls for more Daddy attention.

WARNING FLAG SIX:
Your child, upon receiving "no" from one parent, will go and ask the second parent without telling the second parent that they already received a "no" from the first parent.

Do you remember doing this when you were a kid? One of your parents said, "No," so you went and asked the other parent for permission but did not tell the second parent that the first one said, "No" already. Many kids do this without feeling guilty. This flag is a warning that your child has not been sufficiently trained to the principle of the law, only to the letter of the law. What do we mean by that. He knows the rules but does not know the principle behind the rule. The child is moral on the outside but is not necessarily moral on the inside. Getting a parent to approve the request satisfies the law, which stands above any guiding principle of how permission was gained. There is an outside legal morality but no internal heart morality. This is a warning flag.

WARNING FLAG SEVEN:
Your child shows a declining, instead of an inclining, interest in spiritual things.

The child who shows a declining interest in spiritual things often does so because he knows all about God, but he does not know God. He may have lived off the family's experience of God but not his own.

Here are some healthy indicators of spiritual vitality. Is your child characterized by:

- having quiet times
- using a prayer list
- involvement in ministry service
- appealing to Scripture
- desiring Christian fellowship
- being comfortable with discussions about the Bible
- growing in moral application

Challenge your children to these indicators and do not assume that because they made a profession of faith at five years of age that they are saved. Entertain the possibility that maybe they're not. Maybe it was a group decision in Sunday School but not a true heart change for your child.

SUMMARY
It is fitting that we bring this chapter and series to a close with some final thoughts about *sal-vation*. The word salvation is the all-inclusive word of the gospel. It brings together all the redemptive acts and processes: justification, redemption, grace, propitiation, imputation, forgiveness, sanctification, and glorification. The place where God claims lost people is at the Cross. The Cross is where Jesus died the death that we by all rights should die and would die apart from Him.

Many children raised in Christian communities have a clear knowledge of God but may not know Him personally. They have accepted the concept about God, but not the person of God. Jesus Christ wants your child's heart, not just his head. It is eternally important that you make sure it is not just head knowledge and intellectual assent your son or daughter has given to the Lord. Christ commands a complete surrender of heart and life in order for us to be truly born again. Your child needs to be saved God's way.

Jesus Christ said, "I am the way, the truth, and the life; no one comes to the Father except through me" (John 14:6). The Bible tells us that, "He who has the Son has life; he who does not have the Son of God does not have life" (1 John 5:12). Jesus taught that the truly justified (i.e., the godly) are those who acknowledge their sin and trust in God for forgiveness and His righteousness (John 14:6; Luke 18:9-14; Romans 3:23, 27-28).

Apart from regeneration, the fullness and purpose of life will always be in doubt, and both motive and reality of righteousness are always in question. Positionally speaking, becoming godly is a personal decision, not a parental one. Does your child know the Lord?

Warning Flags Score Sheet

If you have not done it already, add up your test score and compare it to the scale below.

My child's score is _____

Scores

  7 – 9   You're doing great.

10 – 14   You're doing well, but stay watchful of the little behaviors.

15 – 20   A review of *GKGW* wouldn't hurt.

21 – 35   Sign up now for the next *GKGW* class.

Epilogue

The Journey's End

As we wrote our final chapters, we began to realize the significance of the moment. We conclude this series with mixed emotions. Relief, yes, the project is done; now the garden can be weeded. But sadness also. The type that comes when friends say goodbye after having journeyed so long together. Many of you have been with this teaching from the beginning. Expectantly, you sat through *Preparation for Parenting*, then *Preparation for the Toddler Years*, into *Growing Kids God's Way*, then *Reflections of Moral Innocence*, and now through the middle years series.

Although this will not be the last book we write, it will be the last book in this initial series. You are now equipped to be mature and discerning parents of the Faith, rearing God-dependent children, knowing that by your efforts and through your children, God is glorified. We could not have asked for more. Thank you for letting us be part of your family for these many years. Now, go bless the world with your beautiful families showing forth the excellence of Christ.

Maranatha
Gary and Anne Marie

Session One Outline
and Chapters One & Two

Welcome Back

I. Introduction: About This Class

II. The Purpose of This Class

   A. The Five Points

      1. To _____ you and your children for responsible adolescence.
      2. To _____ you to continue with the standard.
      3. To be _____ of this transition period.
      4. To _____ you that this is the last major hill on the road.
      5. To _____ you not to grow weary in well doing.

   B. Course Outline
   Week One:
   Course introduction and review the marks of healthy Growing Kids God's Way families.

   Week Two:
   Deals with the adolescent challenges facing your family, the four levels of maturity, and how parents can bring their children to moral maturity.

   Week Three:
   Influences on your middle years children including moral, physical, and peer pressure.

   Week Four:
   The importance of communicating from the strength of

Notes

your relationship rather than the power of your authority. Practical suggestions on how to talk and listen effectively.

Week Five:
This lesson takes up a number of discipline issues associated with middle years growth and development.

Week Six:
What you should know about dating and courtship before your kids become of age, and a review of the seven warning flags for middle years parents. What to watch out for.

III. Review: What We Are Assuming
    A.   That you are still doing your _____ time.

    B.   That fathers are applying the principles from the Father's _____.

    C.   That you know your child's _____ language.

    D.   That you are consistently giving the _____ reason why.

    E.   That your kids are using the _____.

IV. The Relational Example
    A.   The fifteen traits of healthy *GKGW* families who have teenagers.
        1.   They have a core of shared _____ that all members submit to.
        2.   They know how to _____ with each other.
        3.   They have parents who are not afraid to say, "I was _____."
        4.   They have preteens who can handle _____.
        5.   They have parents who are approachable about their own _____.
        6.   They maintain the marriage as a recognized _____ for family health.
        7.   They make _____ to be with each other and to attend each other's events.

8. They have parents who are not _____ of the teen years.

9. They have teens who are confident of their parents' _____ in them.

10. They have members who are _____ to each other.

11. They have planned family _____.

12. They elevate _____ resolution above conflict avoidance.

13. They have a corporate sense of _____ all members.

14. They swap family _____ for family courtesies as the child matures.

15. They believe the _____ unit is more important than the individual.

B.   Children on "Approach"

Just Ahead:
Adolescence and Maturity

I. Introduction and Review
    A. Defining Terms
        1. Adolescence

        2. Teenager

        3. Youth

    B. What is Adolescence?
        Four levels of maturity
        1. _____ maturity
            Legal maturity is defined by _____ not expe-
            rience, and every nation determines its own legal cus-
            toms and timetable for allowing an individual passage
            into adulthood.

        2. _____ maturity
            Two events mark physical maturity:
            a. The achievement of maximum _____
                growth. (Height).
            b. The ossification of the sacral _____.

        3. _____ maturity
            a. Social maturity refers to one's readiness to be
                an active participant in social policy affecting
                _____ welfare, and the mutual good of
                the society at large. Intellectual maturity speaks
                to the minimum level of intellectual and academic
                attainment necessary to _____ in the
                adult community.

Notes

b. The Law of Social Order.
    The level of social/intellectual maturity required before one can enter the adult community is determined by the _____ or complexity of each society, and the intellectual skills needed to participate as an adult member within the society. Every society sets its own minimum social/intellectual standard that must be met before a person is accepted as an adult. This law affects the _____ of adolescence in each society.

    1) Primitive/Tribal Societies

    2) Pre- and mid-industrial America

    3) Postmodern America

    4) Historical Judaism

4. _____ maturity
    It is natural to think that moral maturity follows the same growth patterns as does physical, social, and intellectual maturity. It is assumed that since a child tends to mature in each of these categories just before entrance into adulthood, that personal morality follows suit. Not so. Such thinking delays moral maturity by removing from parents of pre-adolescents the sense of _____.

    Childhood is the period for imparting moral instruction and directing moral training; but please note carefully that adolescence is the period when principles of right living, thinking, and action should be _____.

II. Understanding Moral Maturity

   A. The Basis of Moral Maturity

      The basis of moral maturity, in a biblical context, is thinking and _____ in harmony with God's Moral Law.

   B. The Key to successful teen-parent relationship

      The key to successful teen-parent relationship is to have an _____ relationship with your children even though he or she is not an adult physically, or intellectually.

   C. For *GKGW* children, the age of moral maturity comes around age _____.

   D. What needs to happen for family harmony in the teen years?

      1. The child must know the _____ of moral truth, not just the how.

         When our values are fashioned by what other people think or what other people will think of us, we gear our message to our children out of otherness _____, rather than the biblical otherness _____. Children then become man-pleasers rather than God-pleasers.

      2. The child must internalize God's _____ as his own.

         Parents must internalize God's _____ as their own.

      3. Parents must live the values they _____.

   E. Facilitating Moral Maturity

      Fear begs for _____ or _____.

      When parents fear the teen years, they either try to control more or surrender in defeat. But it is a matter of fact that when you stop trying to improve your teen and start trying to improve your relationship with your teen, four things happen:

Notes

Notes

1. You put the focus where it rightly belongs on your
   _____.

2. You start parenting by your relational _____
   not your authority.

3. Recognize that each day becomes a _____of accountability.

4. You must press for _____.

Session Three Outline
and Chapters Five & Six

Influences on Behavior

I. Introduction and Review

What is in Your Child's Heart
Philippians 1:10 "Approve that which is excellent."

Key Words:
1. Approve: means test the way of _____
2. Excellent: means _____ and _____.

II. The Influence of Hormones and Body Changes on Behavior
A. Historical View: Hormone/rebellion link

B. The Age of Hormonal Prompting Change

C. The Cause and Effect Link Between Biological Changes and Social Pressures
1. Growing interest in the _____ sex.

2. As a result, preteens become more sensitive to difference between _____ and peers.

3. As a result there begins an indirect effect on parent-child relationship.

III. The Power of Groupthink
A. Groupthink and Development.

The significance of the group
Ages 2-4: The group has very little significance to the child.

Notes

Ages 4-8:   The group has momentary significance. Here and now.

Ages 8-19: The group has great significance to the preteen and teen.

Points to be made about the third phase.
1. During this stage of growth and development, the child moves from an awakening to a full awareness of the significance of the group's _____. That is what brings about peer pressure.

2. Peer pressure is a socializing force that continually challenges the status quo of one's behavior, thinking, and identity association.

3. Peer associations can be both positive and/or negative and therefore will either _____ your family values and relationships or _____ against them.

B. How to Reinforce Your Family's Values While Protecting Your Children from Negative Peer Pressure
1. Power of _____ identity.
    a. Identity defined: Identity is a socializing process by which a person identifies himself with a group he is familiar with, attracted to, or feels empathy with. We derive from our identity associations our sense of belonging and we give back to these associations varying degrees of _____.

    b. Identity, preteens, and healthy families.
        In healthy GKGW families, adolescence is not a time when our children seek a new identity but rather attempt to_____ the one they already have. Any identity crisis for these kids took place at age two, not at fifteen.

2. Power of _____.
    "Community" is a society of families, tied together, sharing common interests, values, and a significant commitment to an ideal, for the mutual benefit of the

individual and the collective membership.

Community serves a corporate sense of "we-ness" that forms the basis of a healthy _____ cause. It connects people of similar convictions, with a sense of corporate responsibility and a sense of purposefulness beyond self and family.

3. Who sits at your city gate?

and Chapter Seven

Communication and Conversation

I.   Introduction and Review
   A.   Understanding the Power of Sanctifying Grace
        Communication of Grace

        1.   _____ grace

        2.   _____ grace

        3.   _____ grace

   B.   Two components of Communication:

        1.   _____

        2.   _____

II. The Ethics of Communication
   A.   Speaking
        1.   Proverbs 15:1 speaks of the _____ of our
             words: "A soft answer turns away wrath, but harsh
             words stir up anger."

        2.   Proverbs 16:21 describes the _____ of our
             words: "The wise in heart will be called prudent, and
             sweetness of the lips increases learning."

        3.   Proverbs 15:33 and 15:20 speaks of the importance of
             _____ words: "A word fitly spoken is like apples
             of gold." "Like one who takes away a garment in cold
             weather and like vinegar on soda, is one who sings
             songs to a heavy heart."

Notes

4. Proverbs 16:24 speaks of the care we should take in selecting _____ words: "Pleasant words are like a honeycomb. Sweetness to the soul and health to the bones."

5. Colossians 4:6 encourages us to employ _____ words: "Let your speech always be with grace, seasoned with salt, that you may know how you ought to answer each one."

6. James 5:12 speaks of our _____ as demonstrated by our words: "But above all, my brethren, do not swear, either by heaven or by earth or with any other. But let your 'Yes' be 'Yes' and your 'No' be 'No' lest you fall into judgment."

B. Listening
   1. Proverbs 18:13 instructs us to listen to _____ facets of an issue before speaking: "He who answers a matter before he hears it, it is folly and shame to him."

   2. Proverbs 18:17 teaches us not to listen to just one _____ of the story: "The first one to plead his cause seems right. Until his neighbor comes and examines him."

   3. Proverbs 1:33 charges us to listen to the voice of wisdom for our own _____: "But whosoever listens to me will dwell safely, and will be secure, without fear of evil."

   4. James 1:19 summarizes with these words of wisdom: "Let everyone be quick to hear, slow to speak," *and as a result,* "slow to anger."

III. The Practice of Communication
   A. Factors Influencing Parent/Preteen Communication
      1. The _____ is ticking down.

      2. Different _____, different needs.

      a.   Adolescent boys tend to feel more comfortable with _____ conversations?

      b.   Adolescent girls tend to feel more comfortable with _____ conversation?

3.   Different _____, different needs.

4.   Birth _____

5.   Parent/Child _____

B. Five "Musts" for Healthy Preteen Communication
    1.   Must create _____ to talk and listen:
       a.   Father talk times
       b.   Mother talk times
       c.   Father/mother talk times
       d.   Family talk times

    2.   Must listen for _____ and intent.

    3.   Must provide for _____ talks.

    4.   Must guard your tongue and _____.

    5.   Must talk and listen with _____.

How to Encourage

I. Introduction and Review

  A. Stay mindful of the difference between _____ and
  _____.

  B. Stay mindful of the four considerations before responding
  to foolishness.

    1. The punishment must fit the _____.

    2. The commonness of the _____.

    3. The _____ of the moment.

    4. The overall _____ of behavior.

  C. Stay mindful of the three levels of _____.

    1. Minor infractions that call for a _____
    reminder.

    2. Infractions that need some _____.

    3. Offenses that call for the full weight of _____.

II. Punishment and Consequences

  A. Punishment/Consequence Graph (Next Page)

    Punishment is used more in the early years; natural and
    logical consequences more during the later years. Please
    note this relationship below.

Notes

PUNISHMENT

CONSEQUENCES

BIRTH   2   4   6   8   10   12   14

B. Understanding the difference

Punishment and natural or logical consequences are not the same thing. Because moral truth is imparted during early childhood, punishment will be used more than natural or logical consequences. Punishment serves a _____ purpose. It communicates to children a value of good and evil by the weight of punishment ascribed to each wrongful act. In contrast, the use of natural and logical consequences in child training does not communicate values. The use of natural and logical consequences has training in personal _____ as a goal.

C. A child's sense of justice is established through punishment not _____. That is why inappropriate under-punishing and over-punishing are immoral acts on the part of the parent.

III. Do's and Don'ts of Motivating Right Behavior
   A. The Do's of encouragement

     1. Encourage by your _____.

     2. Encourage by _____.

     3. Encourage by showing _____.
       a. _____
       b. _____

4.   Encourage by demonstrating moral _____.

5.   Encourage by inviting your kids to work on your _____.

   Benefits:
   a.   It fosters within the relationship a _____ vulnerability.
   b.   It gives your children opportunity to relationally _____ in you.

B.   The "do nots" of encouragement

1.   Do not _____.

2.   Do not use _____ to change behavior that bothers you.

3.   Do not rob your children of the _____ of serving you.

4.   Do not rob your children of the _____ of encouraging you.

IV. Discipline Potpourri
   A.   Correcting personal attitude

   STATEMENT: When dealing with your child's abstract feelings (i.e attitudes) as opposed to concrete behavior, correction comes not solely by trying to _____ the wrong attitude but by elevating and teaching the opposite virtue (Jealousy vs. Contentment).

   B.   Teach your children by concretely showing them tomorrow's consequences for _____ decisions.

   C.   Understand the concept of micro and macro _____.

   D.   Do not _____ to the lowest common denominator.
   E.   Do not say when they do wrong, "I can't _____ you."

Notes

_____
_____
_____
_____
_____
_____
_____
_____
_____
_____
_____
_____
_____
_____
_____
_____
_____
_____
_____
_____
_____
_____
_____
_____
_____
_____
_____
_____

Notes

F. When correcting your kids do not say, "The Bible says," but instead get into the habit of saying: "_____ says," or, "_____ says in His Word."

G. Practical helps for doing _____.

H. The time for _____ is just about over with.

Session Six Outline
and Chapter Ten & Eleven

Dating & Courtship and the Seven Warning Flags

I. Introduction and Review

II. Thoughts on Courtship and Dating
  A. Neither dating nor courtship have a _____ basis.

  B. Dating Defined:
      175 years ago:

      1. Dating defined by Noah Webster of 1828 read: "Knowing the time of happening or to assign a date to an event or letter."

      Today's Definition:

      2. Dating defined by the American Heritage Dictionary 1995 reads: "A social engagement with persons of the _____ sex."

  C. Defining Courtship and Cultural Dating
      1. Courtship is the act of seeking to gain love or affection with a view toward _____.

      2. Cultural dating is a modern social experience allowing teens to have _____ access to a serious male/female relationship reserved for courtship.

  D. Do's and Do nots of Dating
      1. Do not say to your children: "When you're _____, you can date."

Do have timely conversations about the appropriate practice of dating within _____.

2. Do not encourage _____ dating.

Do allow your children to develop healthy male and female _____ friendships.

III. Seven Warning Flags

If you have an eight year old, this test is not going to be as valid as if your child were twelve. But it will still give you some indication that you are headed off track if your score is too high.

For the first seven questions, score yourself and your child based on the following scale. (Question eight is for you, the parent.)

5 = This is very representative of our child.
4 = This is usually representative of our child.
3 = Sometimes this is representative of our child.
2 = This is not usually representative of our child.
1 = This rarely, if ever, is representative of our child.

1. ____ Your child does not follow the family standards outside of your presence (or the presence of others who know and represent your family values).
2. ____ Your child tends to enjoy friends more than his or her own family. He or she is always asking to bring a friend on family activities.
3. ____ The peers your child is attracted to come from homes that do not share your values.
4. ____ You are starting to hear similar negative reports from a number of different people about your child.
5. ____ Although it might be done in a playful way, your child is continually seeking attention from the opposite sex.
6. ____ Your child, upon receiving "no" from one parent, will go and ask the second parent without telling the second parent that they already received a "no" from the first parent.
7. ____ Your child shows a declining, instead of an inclining, interest in spiritual things.

Take a minute to add up your score and compare it to the scale below.

My child's score is _____

Scores
  7 – 9   You're doing great.
10 – 14   Doing well but stay watchful of the little behaviors.
15 – 20   A review of *GKGW* wouldn't hurt.
21 – 35   Sign up now for the next *GKGW* class.

8.   How will you know if you're leading your preteen and teen by your influence or your authority?

    A.   When you parent by your influence, you will _____ with your kids.

    B.   When you parent by your authority, you will have a _____ with your kids.

Notes

Index

More Parenting Resources

by Gary Ezzo, M.A. and Dr. Robert Bucknam, M.D.

With over two million homes to their credit, trusted parenting authors Gary Ezzo and Dr. Robert Bucknam bring their collective wisdom, experience, and insights to bear on this critical phase of growth and development. From first steps to potty training made easy and everything in between, it is all here for you.

ON BECOMING BABYWISE

This book is the first of a six part series that has gained national and international recognition for its immensely sensible approach to parenting a newborn. Coming with the applause of over two million parents and twice as many babies worldwide, *On Becoming Babywise* provides a prescription for responsible parenting. The infant management plan offered by Ezzo and Bucknam successfully and naturally helps infants synchronize their feeding/waketime and nighttime sleep cycles. The results? You parent a happy, healthy and contented baby who will begin sleeping through the night on average between seven and nine weeks of age. Learning how to manage your newborn is the first critical step in teaching your child how to manage his life.

ON BECOMING BABYWISE II

This series teaches the practical side of introducing solid foods, managing mealtimes, nap transitions, traveling with your infant, setting reasonable limits while encouraging healthy exploration and much more. You will learn how to teach your child to use sign language for basic needs, a tool proven to help stimulates cognitive growth and advance communication. Apply the principles and your friends and relatives will be amazed at the alertness, contentedness and happy disposition of your toddler.

ON BECOMING TODDLERWISE

There is no greater fulfillment a parent can receive than the upturned face of a toddler, eyes speaking wonders and a face of confidence in discovering a brand new world with Mom and Dad. In just over a year, the helpless infant emerges as a little moving, talking, walking, exploratory person marked by keen senses, clear memory, quick perceptions and unlimited energy. He emerges into a period of life know affectionately as the Toddler Years. How ready are you for this new experience? The toddler years are the learning fields and you need a trustworthy guide to take you through the unfolding maze of your child's developing world. *On Becoming Toddlerwise* is a tool chest of workable strategies and ideas that multiplies your child's learning opportunities in a loving and nurturing way. This resource is as practical as it is informative.

ON BECOMING POTTYWISE FOR TODDLERS

Potty training doesn't have to be complicated and neither should a resource that explains it. *On Becoming Pottywise for Toddlers* looks to developmental readiness cures of children as the starting point of potty training. Readiness is primary perquisite for successful training according to best selling authors, Gary Ezzo and Pediatrician Robert Bucknam. While no promise can be made, they can tell you that many moms successfully complete their training in a day or two, some achieve it literally in hours. What makes the developmental readiness approach work so successfully?

Timing: Learning to recognize the optimal window for potty training your toddler.

Education: Learning the most effective way to teach your toddler the potty training process.

Motivation: Learning how to instill into your toddler a sustained excitement about using the potty on his or her own.

This resource is filled with time test wisdom, workable solutions and practical answers to the myriad of questions that arise during training.

ON BECOMING PRESCHOOLWISE

Who can understand the mind of a preschooler? You can! Know that above all else, a preschooler is a learner. His amazing powers of reasoning and discrimination are awakened through a world of play and imagination. Through home relationships, he learns about love, trust, comfort, and security; through friends he learns to measure himself against a world of peers; and through unconditional love, a child establishes his own unique selfhood. The growth period between ages three and five years is all about learning, and *On Becoming Preschoolwise* is all about helping parents create the right opportunities and best environment to optimize their child's learning potential. Now influencing over two million homes world-wide, trusted parenting authors Gary Ezzo and Dr. Robert Bucknam once again bring their collective wisdom, experience, and insight to bear on this critical phase of preschool training. From teaching about the importance of play to learning how to prepare a preschooler for the first day of school, from organizing your child's week to understanding childhood fears and calming parental anxiety, sound advice and practical application await the reader. You will find this resource as practical as it is informative, curative as much as it is encouraging.

ON BECOMING CHILDWISE

Ready! Set! Grow! You became a parent overnight...but it takes much longer to become Childwise. Just when you master the baby stage, greater challenges arise. Intellect, self-awareness, curiosity, and social roles are emerging-requiring consistent, caring guidance from you. Equip yourself with more than fifteen Childwise principles for training kids in the art of living happily among family and friends. Foster the safe, secure growth of your child's self-concept and worldview. *On Becoming Childwise* shows you how to raise emotionally balanced, intellectually assertive, and morally sensible children. It's the essential guidebook for the adventurous years from toddler to grade-schooler!

ON BECOMING PRETEENWISE

The middle years, eight to twelve years of age, are perhaps the most significant attitude-forming period in the life of a child. It is during this time that the roots of moral character are established.

From the foundation that is formed, healthy or not-so-healthy family relationships will be built. These are the years when patterns of behavior are firmly established patterns that will impact your parent-child relationship for decades to come. Rightly meeting the small challenges of the middle years significantly reduces the likelihood of big challenges in the teen years. In other words, the groundwork you lay during your child's middle years will forever impact your relationship even long after he or she is grown. Included are discussions related to the eight major transitions of middle years children including how to create a family-dependent and not a peer-dependent child. How to lead by your relational influence and not by coercive authority. What discipline methods work and what methods do not work and how to recognize if your child is in trouble.

ON BECOMING TEENWISE

Why do teenagers rebel? Is it due to hormones, a suppressed primal desire to stake out their own domain, or a natural and predictable process of growth? To what extent do parents encourage or discourage the storm and stress of adolescence? *On Becoming Teenwise* looks at the many factors that make living with a teenager a blessing or a curse. It exposes the notions of secular myth and brings to light the proven how-to applications of building and maintaining healthy relationships with your teens. Whether you worry about your teen and dating or your teen and drugs, the principles of *On Becoming Teenwise* are appropriate and applicable for both extremes and everyone in between. They do work!

ADDITIONAL PARENTING RESOURCES

By Gary Ezzo and Anne Marie Ezzo
Let's Ask Auntie Anne (The Series)

In this series of books we depart from our traditional method of dialectic instruction, (premise, facts, argument and conclusion) and turn to an older and more personal style of persuasion—sharing parenting principles in story-form. Who doesn't love a good story? Stories are entertaining and provide a unique conduit for dispensing practical wisdom and moral truth that otherwise might be lost in an academic venue. When we read or hear a story we find ourselves feeling for the characters through their speech and thoughts. We often identify and empathize with their fears, hopes, dreams and expectations. Most importantly, from their successes and failures we can learn lessons for life. Stories have the power to change us—and indeed they do!

The *Let's Ask Auntie Anne* series consist of five stories and five pertinent parenting themes. Each story is embedded with practical advice that will guide the reader to greater understanding of the complexities of child rearing and hopefully serve as a friend to motivate positive change. The beautiful, historical City of Charleston, South Carolina, frames the backdrop for the series. Auntie Anne draws her parenting lessons from the city's rich history and the daily life of people living on or near the Carolina saltwater marshes. Charleston's glorious past from the Colonial period through the American Revolution, the Civil War, and into the present day and the beauty of its perfectly maintained historical district, cobblestone streets and waterfront parks are all woven into Auntie Anne's lessons.

The descriptions of places, people, scenes, and the anecdotal stories in each book are factual. Apart from Auntie Anne, the characters in our stories are fictional but their needs accurately reflect the many common concerns and challenges for today's parents. The authors speak through Auntie Anne's life story to satisfy the needs of each inquiring couple. Come visit with Auntie Anne. Here you will find a friend, one who connects for a new generation of parents the descriptive—the way it was and the way it is—with the prescriptive—the way it should be.

In Book One, Mac and Vicki Lake can not figure out why their children act as if they are not loved. Mom and Dad are missing something so basic that even the simple phrase "I love you" falls short of its intended meaning. How well did Auntie Anne help them? You decide after reading *How to Raise a Loving Child*.

In Book Two, meet Bill and Elaine Lewis. Who doesn't know at least one family facing the frustration of irresponsible children? Messy rooms, wet towels on the floor, and unfinished homework are just the beginning. Join Bill and Elaine as they go with Auntie Anne on a journey to the heart of *How to Raise a Responsible Child*.

In Book Three, little do Rick and Lela Harvey know that a lack of security is the root of their children's behavioral problems. Nervous, irritable children acting out at school in seemingly uncontrollable ways are a dead giveaway. Auntie Anne's has a plan for this home. Find out what and who needs to change in *How to Raise a Secure Child*.

In Book Four, Clarke and Mia Forden seek out Auntie Anne's advice on building trusting relationships. For Clarke and Mia, the pace of today's family is troubling. How will fathers capture the hearts of their children with so little time? Find out what they wished they had learned a dozen years earlier in *How to Raise a Trusting Child*.

In Book Five, Geoff and Ginger Portier tell their story of how Auntie Anne taught them how to make virtues and values real in the lives of their children. What will it take to create a love for moral beauty within the heart of their children? Auntie Anne provides solid answers in *How to Raise a Moral Child*.